José Ferrer de Couto, Charles Kirchhoff

**Cuba May Become Independent**

A Political Pamphlet Bearing upon Current Events

José Ferrer de Couto, Charles Kirchhoff

**Cuba May Become Independent**
*A Political Pamphlet Bearing upon Current Events*

ISBN/EAN: 9783337102524

Printed in Europe, USA, Canada, Australia, Japan

Cover: Foto ©ninafisch / pixelio.de

More available books at **www.hansebooks.com**

# CUBA

# MAY BECOME INDEPENDENT.

A POLITICAL PAMPHLET BEARING
UPON CURRENT EVENTS:

BY

DON JOSE FERRER DE COUTO,

CHIEF OF CIVIL ADMINISTRATION, &c., &c.

TRANSLATED FROM THE SPANISH

BY

CHARLES KIRCHHOFF,

Former Consul of Prussia at San Francisco (California),
Translator of "General Instructions for Consuls
of the German Empire," and Commercial
Editor of EL CRONISTA, &c., &c.

NEW YORK.
"EL CRONISTA" PRINTING OFFICE.
1872.

# DEDICATION.

THE work I have published is dedicated to Americans of the North, to those of Central and South America, to loyal as well as to disloyal Cubans.

In thus addressing myself to the entire New World, dedicating them this work, the confidence which inspires me is not a slight one. But do not think that presumptuous vanity dictates the course I have taken. Having spent five-and-twenty years of the better portion of my life in studying the relations and interests of the hemisphere of Columbus towards the rest of the world, I believe that I may be permitted to raise a voice, where there are people who claim a proficiency, although they be but superficially familiar with science, and although they never entered the portals where science is taught.

And I may, furthermore, aspire to dedicate this work to the New World in general in the name of my native country, for the New World in general, even more than my country, may be benefitted by the inferences to which the study leads.

Americans of the North will note, that the question has a bearing on both their finances and on their commercial relations, even though the consideration of right and morality were not made to weigh in the balance.

Those of Central America will note, that it is in their

interest that morality and right be not the losers within the Mexican Gulf.

Those of South America are interested in the independence of Central America being kept intact.

Cubans, that are loyal, will all the better measure the great service which this loyalty renders to the future and glory of their native land, to its commercial relations with North America, to the consolidation of both Central and South America, to right and morality in the New World at large.

Disloyal Cubans will open their eyes and act accordingly; for if four years of strife and intrigue have sufficed to stop for ten years at least advancement in the Island, in a struggle, which Spain is able to prolong indefinitely by virtue of her resources, of her power, and of the strength of a legitimate cause, it certainly would seem preferable that the goal they aspire to reach be attained by the peaceful progress of half a century, rather than that in twenty years the Island recede to those days of primitive colonization, in which, alas! Hayti and St. Domingo, are vegetating at the present day.

If you wish to find the key that is to set at rest the questions here involved, read the pamphlet in a spirit of impartiality, the same spirit which presides over them, and with this *Dixi*.

JOSE FERRER DE COUTO.

# PREFACE.

FEW questions ventilated in the world in times past and present have brought to the surface and fostered a greater amount of errors than the Cuban. Not only have these misconceptions arisen from the heated imagination of some natives of Cuba, not only have they crept into the calculation of those, who covet the possession of the jewel as a great job, but even into the minds of men have they been instilled, who may be put down as impartial judges, and who, nevertheless, have not, in studying the question, gone sufficiently to the bottom of a problem of the first magnitude, calling for a thorough sifting.

We have, therefore, in the columns of EL CRONISTA penetrated into the question to the extent of our capacities, so that public opinion may judge by the light of truth, impelled as we were by the regret, that gross misconception long prevailing on the subject should still cling to it, and although we know that much of what we brought forward was not built on quicksand, much, we are sorry to confess, remains to be done to triumphantly and radically refute errors, and those who, in one way or another, are interested in the question, have a right to claim a thorough elucidation of it.

But it chances to be that journalism, of all the agents of modern civilization, is the most impressionable, the least

# CAN CUBA BECOME INDEPENDENT ?

UNDER this so significant heading the *El Emigrado* has published an article, which we shall copy in full, instead of giving extracts therefrom, for it contains nothing but what will answer our purposes:

" There are few questions, which more prominently preoccupy the thoughts and sentiments of our readers than the one which heads these lines, cursory as the may be, but sincere, for the possibility of Cuban independence, has been to nearly all of us a subject of favorite study, of deep meditation, of heartfelt desire; a cause of unheard-of sacrifices; a basis of titanic labors and of the most vehement and incessant aspirations.

" With ourselves it has been at once a subject, a cause, a basis and an aspiration. It has been no less attractive to us, no less urgent with us, no less firm and no less sure and constant than what it has been to any of those who may honor us with an attentive perusal of these lines. The solution of that, which to many is still a problem, has now been greatly simplified by ruthless experience, by the stern teaching of facts; let us study the question, therefore, in its main features, and let that which happened be our luminous beacon, which may lead the opinion of those to a safe anchorage, who know to subordinate all sentiment to the safety of our native land, of those who, as we ourselves do believe, that it is the duty of every Cuban of honor to save Cuba at all risks, although he perish in its attainment, and although his days may be embittered by vociferous patriotism, that judges from outside appearances and faints before the arduous labor of penetrating into the essence of things.

"We have said that Cuban emigrants, whose faithful echo we are, ask: *Can Cuba become independent?* we shall add at once that this question has become a matter of fact, imperceptible as it was at first—because enthusiasm stifled it—that it has become more generally mooted, that it has been openly pronounced, and that it now most legitimately pre-occupies those, who in good faith take an interest in our beloved Island. This is an undeniable truth; we have discovered it, and claim no greater credit for it, than that we bring to public notice a fact already notorious, though some may call it lukewarmness, some weariness, and want of faith others. With us there is no such thing. We call it an awakening from deep slumbers; we call it a noble wish to get at the truth by all means; we applaud the question, and we esteem those, who in their zeal to learn that which is true, leave the easy paths that lead to the castle-in-the-air which is called the palace of popularity.

"Let us cast aside with disdain all vacillation, unworthy of manly breasts, and let us attack in front this question like any other—*Can Cuba become independent?* Let us examine into the matter, let us give substance to convictions by lending them the binding power of an indestructible argument.

"To ask whether Cuba can become independent, a question which is now being raised by nearly all our brethren, is tantamount to doubting that such independence can be accomplished. That which in itself carries the august stamp of truth will shine forth by its own strength, it requires no demonstration, it is because it exists, and it exists because it is. It enters nobody's mind to attempt impugning it. But when the sentiment is alive and yet wavering and turning within a vicious circle, when it has but a faint perception of truth, or seems to seek it, but to avoid it, when it shrinks from the logical examination of consequences, to which the very arguments it has raised lead it, it may be truly said, that the thought itself is afraid of its own wanderings, that it knowingly tends to surround itself with darkness, and that imagination and hope strive to betray a stern judgment, that doubt is the commencement, involuntary and unconscious though it may be, of a negation, which only waits to take form by a daring spirit pronouncing it.

"Let it be known, then, that in this moral agony, fertile in torments greater than those with which the imagination of a Dante peopled the infernal regions, our brethren are living for a twelve month past. Let us appeal to their noble hearts, let us knock at the portals of their conscience to ask them whether or not we speak the truth? And if this be so, resolved as we are to carry the whole load of truth which has fallen upon our weak shoulders, we shall concentrate all our energy to pronounce the negation, which we poor emigrants anticipate, and which nobody has the boldness to speak out publicly.

"Let us be sincere, let us be frank, let sentiment be hushed, let us stifle the wish by the call to reason, let sentiment be always subordinate to the counsels of true, of sound patriotism, and though ingratitude and calumny poison our very existence, let us deny that which, logically, cannot be upheld.

"No, Cuba cannot become independent; let us not shrink from recognizing that much, for the acknowledgment is in conformity with that, which a straightforward criticism will discover, and the further spilling of precious blood may yet be avoided, which would uselessly water fields of battle instead of nourishing our beloved country with its enlivening and generous sap.

"What elements does our Island possess for conquering independence? None, in truth, but the indomitable valor of its great sons. But valor will not of itself suffice, where the opponent is as valiant and has at his disposal resources of every kind, an organization that cannot be unhinged, and a tenacity of purpose not inferior to our own. But valor saves honor, and in Cuba honor has been saved. Nor will valor suffice to change the essence of society, to reconstruct the basis of its public life, to attain the manhood of political efficacy and to assume a place among the nations of the earth.

"Valorous is Ireland, valiant are the Southern States of the American Union, and yet their military bravery, shown on a hundred battle-fields, has not given them the independence which they are sighing for. Material bravery is crushed by material obstacles, and when these have proved victorious, moral bravery has to be appealed to hardly less frequent, and even sublimer in order to tie up the wounds of a bleeding country. There is no dishonor in having been beaten from the moment the resistance has been glorious, and bravery is not made merely that we should satisfy our aspirations, but to lend it towards the greatest good of that which we defend.

"But admitting even that by prodigious efforts we

wrung from Spain the wished-for independence, are we so very certain, that we could live the life of an independent nation? To conquer is difficult, but it is a thousand times more difficult to retain and proserve. Supposing, then, we were independent, are we sure that we can bring together the elements that are requisite to make use of that which we conquered? Shall we, in cutting loose from a government which ruled us during centuries, understand how we shall be capacitated to govern ourselves in the centuries to come? Another question here arises which can neither be solved to our satisfaction.

"The drift of the present revolution and that which we have written about it in our last three editions with the approbation of our readers, go to show clearly that we are not permitted to hope for such a consummation. Although born with superabundant elements, we have seen the insurrection flicker away by degrees, and our heart has been crying blood, on discovering that the greatest stumbling-block to success had to be searched for in the unbridled ambition of our leaders, the bad faith of our allies, the want of respect between equals, and consideration bestowed on inferior men. With rare, very rare exceptions we have seen real merit unheeded and the gift of intrigue exalted: the management of the public good has run at random, the laws that were made have not been a curb on the man invested with power, while they were made to weigh down the powerless; and if these undeniable facts have occurred during the revolution, at a time when our resources were over-abundant, what are we entitled to hope for under ordinary circumstances, in which we have lacked the magnanimity to sacrifice our ambition to our duties while our country was endangered, when everything should have impelled us to unite in that which we strove to attain. And this is not only the history of yesterday, it is that of to-day, and while we gave its outlines, we endeavored to bring down our judgment within the spirit of toleration inseparable from truth itself.

"Up to this point we have demonstrated, though it be with deep regret that the Island of Cuba cannot cut loose from Spanish tutelage through her own making, and that recent events raise grave doubts as to our knowing how to place on a fair basis our independence were we to obtain it. But what shall we say further from the moment that we seriously begin to weigh the dangers which would surround Cuba, were we to go begging for our independence at the hands of foreign help.

"No allies need we look for outside of Cuba to accomplish political emancipation, for there are none, and those that may be found, are either impotent or obnoxious. And even admitting this to be saying too much, what foreign nation came to our assistance during the present insurrection? Some men in South America, in a timid manner within government circles, to such a point that the assistance was impracticable, and outside of these circles there were expressions of sympathy, which, though they rejoiced our hearts, had no practical effect as to the end to be reached. From other quarters adventurers have joined us, on bad terms as they were, with the general peace of mankind, and who have been the disowned of the revolution.

And do not let us speak of the United States, for the blindness would be unpardonable to still believe in the genuineness of their loudly proclaimed friendship for the Cuban people. The United States have lured us to believe in help and did not lend the assistance, and they are the only nation that possesses power enough in America to make its will respected, a nation by tradition the enemy of Spain. Who gave refuge to our revolutionary 'juntas' and allowed military expeditions to slip out, violating in permitting a l this to be done international law to please us? Away with the b oody farce here enacted! Of what use has the harboring of our 'juntas' been but to breed an end'ess element of discord, of what use have the expeditions really been beyond transferring money to the pockets of our *determined protectors ?'"

"We have previously stated, and shall not get tired of repeating it, the protection of the United States is nothing but a means of bleeding both Spain and Cuba, so that at a given moment the American Union may all the easier seize the coveted prize. Has not the great argument invariably been the eventual possession of Cuba, the key to the Mexican Gulf, whenever public men of theirs have spoken on the subject, and whenever the press has thundered in favor of Cuban liberty, and all this without tacit or expressed reservation? To assist us has not been their aim, but rather that we should perish and that Cuba should be at the mercy of the punic faith of our *generous allies.*

"Let Cuba be independent to-morrow, and in a short time the fable of the wolf and the lamb would at her expense be re-enacted, for our beloved Island would be found disturbing the waters of the gulf which bathes the feet of the American Union.

"The events now transpiring abundantly prove that we

should in no case obtain our independence without passing through a desperate struggle and even admitting that we issued from it victoriously, our resources would be at an end. Picture to yourselves, then, our country bled to death and handed over in its internal workings to the convulsive machinations of its own ambitious chiefs, how and with what should we begin another war, not any more with Spain, but with the most pugnacious power of America, with a nation, whose basis of operations would be at ten hours' distance from our shores. We should either succumb to the blow of Attila, or we should convert our country into a closed tilt-ground for Latin and Saxon influence to fight its battles in, our liberty being forfeited in any event, though acquired at such cost.

"The whole problem as to whether Cuba can become independent, to our regret is, therefore, narrowed down to the inevitable dilemma: Either Cuba will be what she now is, more or less free, but preserving intact her social physiognomy, such as her idiosyncracy is constituted within the folds of the Latin family, or she will from internecine anarchy be handed over a slave to the foreign tyrant, that would blot out her very name, would expel her sons, and would finally surrender her as a prey to its proconsuls and a victim to northern civilization, that substitutes guns for the constitution, the revolver to the plough, and the adoration of degrading material interests to that of the God of catholicism.

"In other words the whole thing resolves itse'f into this—'*In order to be Cuba, Cuba cannot be independent.*'

"This is the truth, which we record with deep regret, but which reason dictates to us through the teachings of disappointments. If we have swerved from the truth, let our friends lead us back to the strict facts of the case, let them correct our errors, for that which we wish to discover, is their greatest good. If on the other hand we are right, if we have been truthful interpreters, as in good conscience we do believe, of that which Cuban emigrants feel and think, if in doing so, we have lent consistency to vague and indecisive opinions, let them cut loose without further hesitation from the false patriots, who strive to mislead them, in order to swindle them out of their daily bread, in earning which they do credit to themselves and to their country, the false patriots, who may fling the poisoned arrow of slander at us, if they think fit that we should be singled out to be the victim for daring to perform an act of public virtue, which their own demoralization would probably shrink from performing.

We ourselves, humble workmen of intelligence and progress, are content to serve Cuba in the paths of truth, the fountain of all justice. While the penalty of unpopularity does not deter us, nor popularity entice us, threats do not frighten us, for as long as that which we strive to propagate is just, it will vanquish with the help of good men. And although this address of ours may prove a fountain of annoyances to us, the divine promise will both console and strengthen us: '*Happy are those who thirst for justice, for they shall be satisfied.*'"

Referring to the foregoing article, we beg to state that we differ from *El Emigrado* in the definitive conclusion which he arrives at, *Cuba on the contrary can become independent*, and although this sentence of ours may seem strange, it has nevertheless for its basis former periodical labors of ours, and it is our intention, to devote a series of articles to the subject, beginning with the ensuing week. In publishing them the utmost attention will be bestowed on the arguments we shall bring to bear upon the questions to be ventilated.

## CUBA MAY BECOME INDEPENDENT.

### I.

> Spain colonizing the New World did not intend to perpetuate herself in her colonies, but in the history of universal civilization.—Examples which justify her conduct.—Evils of the premature emancipation of the Spanish-American republics.—Cuba compared with said republics.—Her progress in relation to those of the Peninsula.—Erroneous opinion that is alleged about this matter.—Rectification.—Origin of the ideas on which these articles are founded.—Vouchers.—Invocation to the impartiality of those who read this work, in order that they may be able to judge it.

HOW so? Have the insurgent Cubans, or those who are loyal, really supposed, that Spain would ever, and to the day of judgment, strive to retain the precious Island? Can any sane man suppose, that such a thing is or will be the purpose of Spain?

Reflect on the destinies we have fulfilled and still to accomplish! Nations that have carried out missions on earth, such as we have filled in the history of civilization, live for ever, although not within the precincts of any given landmarks beyond their natural limits, for they will stay there but the time which their mission has prescribed, so that they may hand back the colonies to universal society shaped to its level, sufficiently developed and in the age of manhood.

So did Rome, and thus did Greece. Carthage had the same aim, but for the good fortune of her antagonists. Primitive populations, which they converted into colonies, in due time sallied forth to participate in the existence of fertile and natural independence.

Spain sent forth the great contingent of her sons for the same purpose, she instilled the fecundating sap of her life into virgin America and the nations, that arose, sprang from her life blood. Had these young nati us been less precipitate in striving to emancipate themselves, too young as they were, how very different would not their future be at the present day, how much greater their real importance in the general conclave of self-constituted nations.

Cuba, the youngest sister of them all, fully proves the truth of what we bring forward. She was content to be kept tenderly sheltered near the bosom of her mother, and in doing so, attained greater culture, greater wealth, a more perfect development, with a future in prospect superior to the one that smiled or will ever smile per hance upon the others.

With what generous ideas, what sublime sentiments, with what gushing love and kindness, with what abnegation and tenderness has not Spain striven to support her favorite daughter while she followed in the path of civilization at a great distance from herself!

In Cuba, even ahead of the Spanish Peninsula, steam was applied to communication on shore and afloat, and thus setting an example to Latin America. How many years ahead of the most civilized from among the Spanish American Republics did not the steam-whistle sound its echo across the fields and along the shores of our Island, steam, the most useful and fertile invention which the ages have witnessed, in positive good to mankind?

Some will answer, that Cuba owed to the vicinity of the United States this advantage, and not to the happy condition in which Spain kept the Island. But as near at hand is the Mexican Republic, and yet, not one railway line is finished there to the present day, not a single merchant steamer has been built in Mexico, or even carries the Mexican flag.

And besides, were the United States the only nation that applied steam to industry? Did not England, Belgium, France, Russia and Germany and the whole European continent snatch up the new motive power with feverish haste and improve its application in an astonishing manner? And if in the face of all these facts the Spanish Peninsula caused her favorite daughter to take the lead among all the Spanish countries in this valuable acquisition, is not this another positive proof of the love she bore her, of the zeal, with which unmistakably she strove to develop the Island, so that Cuba might attain the age of emancipation a model of well-ruled colonies, of well trained nationalities, of nations in full maturity and sufficiently strong to make front against a host of pit-falls?

Some may be inclined to think, that the spirit of our present argumentation is a forced and transitory one, that it is not bound up with our national sentiments, as we pretend it is. In order to dispel such a grave error, all we have to do, is to point back towards the labor, we have been pursuing during near y seven years. Suffice it to say, that the same ideas were uppermost in our mind at the time of assuming the management of this new paper, that we did so in connection with the Government at Madrid, and that all other suppositious are, therefore, utterly groundless.

And on thus taking charge of *La Crónica*, the glorious base and foundation of EL CRONISTA, which we fear will never equal its predecessor, we made public our programme and one of its passages bore the following sentence:

"The reincorporation of Santo Domingo within the folds of the mother-country, turned as it came to be into a cry of alarm sent forth to Spanish America by our common enemies, has been an over-stepping of the ordinary rule which Spain had laid down for its general conduct towards the Republics of the new continent. A group of our family there precariously existed, not only because torn by domestic discord, but because under constant threat of a savage enemy, then making preparations to destroy our brethren by sword and fire.

"Spain, the noble and glorious Spain, comprehending the strategical importance of the country, not that she coveted its possession, for it presented on its face nothing but additional expenses, but in its bearings upon the immense future *of the Great Empire of the Spanish Antilles,* which human progress in all its manifestations would have to lift into existence in due course of time, *and much to the liking of Spain,* in the world of Columbus, the same as Great Britain arose facing the old continent under less auspicious circumstances."

Our readers will do us the justice to believe, that at the critical moment of making our programme in a paper supported by the National Government we could not well have undertaken to venture upon a sentence of this kind on our own responsibility, for there was near at hand a most enlightened minister who represented with dignity the Spanish interests.

No, we did not speak at the time, of our own accord, we wrote that, which the Government at Madrid thought, that which at the same time was blended with our own sentiments, that which all Spain cherishes with joyfulness.

And are not the words, we have quoted, sufficiently explicit such as they are and of a nature to silence those, who attack what we say? Hear, then, the amplified sense, which we attributed to them in a leader, in *La Crónica*, dated 30th December, 1865, the same year, in which we assumed the editorship of the paper.

"The Antilles have their destiny written in golden letters on the book of humanity. Their mission is one of greatness and glory still, as sentinels and shields of the Spanish-American Continent, under the banner of their discoverers. And the hand of God shall trace out to them new paths in the march of universal civilization, and when their vital forces shall possess cohesion enough by virtue of greater maturity and development, they will reach the natural destiny, awaiting nations, that rear a new life, *Spain will frankly assist them to that end, she will lend them efficacious and generous help,* so that they may with dignity represent the better portion of our race in Spanish America and enter the lists of *independent nations,* linked with imperishable ties of true love to the *illustrious matron, who thus introduces them to the world"*

Let what we have said suffice for the day as a forerunner to the labor we have undertaken and let those, who seek the truth in good faith read calmly and without prejudice. The question in hand is too important, no less than the life or death of a people is here involved, and certainly a couple of hundred of stubborn men are not the arbiters, to solve in a fit of passion that which in family conclave should be judged upon mature investigation, giving due weight to the general interests tied up with problems of such nature.

## II.

Synthesis of the previous article.—Its natural consequences cannot prescind from any of the details which contribute to form its antecedent propositions.—Application of this axiom to the development of colonial populations.—Demoralization of politics and the deplorable influence they thus exercise in practice.—The same argument is also applicable to the final aim of this treatise.—Doubts as to its being of any effect against the pretended wisdom of positive ignorance.—Firm resolution to go on with the treatise and to combat error, convinced that the reader will not knowingly be misled by the latter.

Taking up the thread of our previous article, which was intended to be a preamble of this thesis, three important problems appear solved already from the very start, to wit: That the colonizing nations are not perpetuated *ad eternum* in the populations, which civilization has handed over to them and yet are not within the limits traced out by nature to their own territory, that *La Crónica*, the basis upon which EL CRONISTA was reared thus understood the subject and thus interpreted the same on being consigned to our management, that the Antilles have before them an immense future as a providential nationality, independent and perhaps indeed, holding the balance between races in the New World, that the government at Madrid has been imbued with the idea and still entertains it, not by virtue of events more or less fovorable or deplorable, but by reason of the eminently paternal calling delegated to the governments of the world, the vulgar spirit notwithstanding, which has undertaken to analize the bearings of the case and believes and preaches the reverse, rendering impossible the administration of public order, were we to listen to it.

The case as it stands is a clearly defined one, consequently, and everything would point in the affirmative with reference to the theme of our articles. But can the aims of a government having for their object civilization and humanity be allowed to be thwarted with impunity in their process of elaboration, and when thus hampered, will not the attainment of its aims be crippled, however much the human family may wish it success?

No human power, indeed, can with impunity disturb the harmony of the great conceptions, which have the spirit of God for their source, and there is the same difference between the measured steps of nature in its developments and the improvisation of an artificial state of affairs, as exists between the sublime and the coarse, the same which distinguishes man in his utmost perfection from the unborn babe; we have here indeed the most eloquent and proud contrast which may be thrown into the faces of the pride of some individuals, so that they may not reproduce the scene of Luzbel, to the evident dismay of the world's progress and of the manifest destiny of their country.

With politics, if we may be permitted to make some digressions, though bearing upon the subject, people have been so much familiarized, that we can hardly meet with a person, who does not handle them and deem them the easiest thing, despite the difficulty of this complicated science, and since this chances to be the case, not a day of peace is safe among men, nor is there a nook or corner, exempt from danger and innovation.

Politics are despoiled now-a-days of the prestige, which surrounded them, when they were exclusively wielded by eminent statesmen, by men, who had grown grey in their study, bent down under the experience of a laborious life in their service and commanding respect at the hands of the masses, whereas at the present day the barefacedness is great, indeed, with which their most arduous problems are discussed and disposed of by men of a deficient grasp of mind and education and but too often vulgar in sentiment.

Who does not deem himself capacitated to-day, to govern the nation from which he sprang; who has not the ambition to do the best he can, the most moral and the most honorable, so that his country may gain credit thereby, that its material well-being may be perpetuated, that its fame and prestige may rise?

And how many did not seize the reins of State power with similar honorable intentions, anxious to serve their country, to be precipitated shorn of glory from the pedestal, which supererogation caused them to mount in an hour fatal to themselves?

It would seem that the majority of those who handle politics, be it in the open air or from the tribune, in Parliament or in the newspapers, think that all that is required are certain disconnected definitions, to assume a coloring of one doctrine or another, to seize with enthu iasm one opinion or another more or less adapted to the nature of the ground where it is to be brought into play, in order to stamp them the most consummate judges of the art, unheedful of the warnings of their most loyal opponent, from the moment that their illusions are in the least interfered with.

We have been obliged to make this digression, because we apprehend that we shall stumble upon these doctors of the faith of modern id-as from the moment that we pronounce the word that *Cuba may become independent*, after deeply studying this complicated question in all its features. From their point of view the logic of time and things is nothing but a reactionary pre occupation, they will attempt to haul down our most cherished conclusions, should they not chime in with theirs, although nothing inspire their motives in doing so but caprice, nothing but a thoughtless obstinacy, evidently exaggerated as it may be.

We furthermore apprehend, that their inexpert followers, equally se f-sufficient and who will endorse anything akin to their ideas, will attack our arguments merely because preceding from the opposite side, without reason and without investigation, believing, as they seem to do, that they need not trouble themselves about anything concerning the welfare of the people beyond the present generation, that men should weigh their own individual interests first and those of their country at large afterwards.

But, however, this may be, that which we have undertaken, shall, with the help of Providence be accomplished to the extent of our capacities and in trying to do so we shall soon see, with what degree of favor or disfavor our reasonings will be received at the hands of those who, while opposed to us, have never as yet taken the trouble of going to the bottom of the question to be ventilated.

We shall, therefore, at our leisure endeavor to throw the fullest light upon it from the various points of view which may be deemed requisite for its thorough elucidation.

## III.

The practical and scientific character of the question.—Sophisms and errors.—They vanish or are explained. The so-called natives of the Island.—The aborigines. —The Spaniards.— Mutual relations. —Respective rights.—Abberrations resulting from denying the one and the others.—General ideas of society as applied to family.—Attributes of home rule.—Limitation by the simple process of time.—Application of the rule to the project of *Cuban independence.*—Divergent opinions as to time and opportunity.—Practical impediments to premature individual and social independence.---Why Cuba sooner than any other colony should fortify her position and future ere striving for independence.—Favorable and adverse hypothesis with reference to her present condition and the one towards which she tends.

Although eminently scientific, the question which we propose to investigate, is not the less practical and we could not well proceed a single step in it, without first trying to remove subtleties and errors, which have arisen in the minds of visionary people and with which they endeavor to bolster up fancied rights.

The generality of seditious Cubans found the ligitimacy of their rebellious action, as proclaimed by them, precisely on the idea of a right which in itself is fictitious, absurd and baseless, because it completely and absolutely denies positive rights.

They pretend to say, that Cuba belongs to them, and not to Spain; according to their notions they are the real and only sons of the country, that the Spaniards are grasping foreign interlopers and the theories thus flippantly enunciated are so hollow, that they will not stand for a moment the search of common sense.

The Cubans would in fact be the sons of the Island, had they descended from the Indians whom the Spaniards found on landing. But since the native race was soon extinct, too weak as it was, from the moment it came in contact with another more powerful and in every respect superior race, it is evident, that those, who proclaim themselves owners of the Island because of their birth on its soil, neither have, nor can have any greater right to it, than the one they have inherited from their fathers, the same Spaniards whom they call grasping foreign interlopers. In order to divert a question so plain and pertinent of every metaphysical argument, all we have to do is to take into consideration that while there are many families in the Island, who by time and successive generations are materially severed form continuity of descendency, there are others, who form the majority, and who have sprung direct from laborious, worthy and honorable Spaniards, who have reared families, are still alive and still preside over them.

Where shall we be landed, however, were we to go and proceed still further in metaphysical deductions and from a question of right pass to a practical and formal solution, sanctioning the theory that property is exclusively bound up with birth and not with the person, that created it; what would the natives of the land do with their fathers, the direct or indirect sons of Spaniards, were they to proceed in the same sense and to defend, not any more the indisputable rights of the mother country, but that over their own properties, acquired by economy, industry and labor?

One of two moral and civil aberrations would have to happen, either the sons would have to drown in the blood of their fathers natural and acquired rights, or, by an act of pity, the fathers, should they issue victoriously from the struggle, would take into tutelage their own sons thus resorting contrary to nature to an anti-social state of affairs, deplorable and not creditable to their sons.

As it chances that society is the natural reflex of family, the question of right may be reduced to a still clearer definition: Is the right to the possession of the father's home claimed by the son more perfect because the son was born in it and superior to that of the father who built it and who declines to leave it till he dies a natural death?

Those who carry to the utmost extremes the artifices of argument say that the rights of the mother country have also their limitations, that it is certain that if on the one hand human society is reflected in the family and that the simile of fathers and sons is pertinent to the question, the laws of nature have, on the other hand, also provided and laid down in the law books of every civilized nation, the emancipation of the individual, and that consequently it is equally applicable to nations.

This argument certainly is not devoid of logic and our opponents will admit that we do not withhold weapons from them, wherewith to sustain their abstractions. But, as with reference to the question to be ventilated, it is not denied, nor ever will be denied *that Cuba may become independent* in good season, other and important problems may be deduced therefrom, which should be mathematically solved, for they remove the question from investigations of absolute right and narrow it down to one of absolute practicability, as has been hinted at by us at the head of this article.

Who, indeed, can determine the majority of age of a colony, its capacity for independent nationality without recurring to mathematical investigations that solve the great economical problems of its nature and its vitality?

Does it suffice, that some excited spirit, impatient to step into the plenitude of perfect liberty, proclaim such majority, while other more reflecting spirits, who may possess more experience in examining questions of this nature, declare, that the state of perfection which the other party believed to have been reached, is mere illusion?

Nothing, indeed, seems more natural, than that the sons should wish to move about in the world by themselves and in a state of independence, but it is quite as natural, that the fathers should place their veto upon a premature independence. How many sons do not condemn the unreflecting weakness of their fathers, who in order not to curb their inclinations, permitted them to sally forth ere the proper time had arrived, only that they might prove a nuisance to good society, a scourge of lawlessness and a blot on a fair name!

The independence of populations reared in the colonial state, as we have them in Cuba, requires certain qualities, in order to render it useful, practical and permanent, not only to themselves, but to others, whose interests are intertwined with theirs, so that the acquisition may prove a positive good, instead of entailing disastrous consequences, discrediting and obliterating it.

And Cuba, more than any other people, sprung from Spaniards in America, should first of all consolidate and fortify the position, which is to raise her to national independence and not to be merely the football or the prey of any other nation. Her office will be to shield her sisters and to command respect by her organization, her wealth and her judgment, by the instrumentality of material and moral strength. She shou'd be in full mastery of the dangers that lie hidden below the heterogeneous population she harbors, the dangers, besides, which are inseparable from her extreme youth, her want of political education, of experience and of routine in State matters.

What use would Cuba be able to make of it on conquering her independence by the means and under the circumstances which the insurgent Cubans propose to employ or create? Would she be able to create an homogeneous state of affairs among individuals there residing; would she lend order and cohesion to parties that are inexorable already in their disputes among each other; would the labor question be practically and beneficially solved; would her riches be developed sufficiently to attract the necessary immigration; would foreign capital be safe, would general commerce be benefitted, taking her start from the present day such as the Island is constituted under the protection of Spain in all its relations of life; would she go on increasing in due proportion to the happy state of independence, as the whole world would naturally be led to hope? Or, would she rather stand stripped by a struggle of her most vital, of her most valuable elements, now abounding on her fortunate soil, torn by a war of races or by discordant political elements, the strongest hands emancipated from labor, with the fountains of her proverbial riches choked, capital flying to more inviting regions, another spectacle the counterpart of Hayti. Wi l she, overcome by weariness, then surrender herself to the strongest nation that may snatch up the prize and thus by a degrading process be transferred from the loving bosom of a mother to slavery, to *grasping foreign interlopers*, indeed, who would use her as a stepping stone from whence the extinction of the whole Spanish-American race would be consummated, because in her national independence she was ncapable of accomplishing more elevated destinies?

Reflect, then, that such may be the fate of Cuba, that her own sons are those who most desire and preach it, and that through their action they may bring it about. And how can we in thus reflecting, prevent bitter irony from conjuring up in our minds maledictions on the heads of the corruptors of modern society, of those who preach the right of whatever individual to outstep the limits, within which an honorable, perchance modest position kept him, so that he may become a man of politics and lead his country to such a state!

But, do not let us be carried away; the material, which we have to go through is vast and complicated, nor can we lose more time, since the painful solution is being fought out by sword and by word.

## IV.

Positive foundations, which should underlie a society aspiring to become independent.—Transitory struggle.—General conformity.—The other phase with the disasters it involves.—Different features attending submission of one nation to another.—Italy ere it was united.—Poland before its dismemberment.—Cuba in her various phases, ancient and modern.—Character of the Peninsular group in the Island.—The creoles of the Island.—Distinction of the Cuban question from those of Mexico and Spanish-America.—Proofs.—Logical deduction in favor of the treatise.

In order to determine the proper moment, at which a colony sprung from the same nationality that founded it, has reached the requisite ability for assuming a state of independence, it will be necessary above every thing else that the principle does not admit of discussion between the great bodies that constitute it. But there may be divergence on the part of the nation which founded the colony.

Not always is a nation resigned to be deprived of part of its territory and in such a case the emancipation of a colony is seldom carried out without an appeal to arms on the part of the mother country with reference to the question raised, in order to prevent its consummation. But from the moment all voices are unanimously raised in support of the colony, thus lending to the latter that moral strength, which does not yield, justice steps forward regardless of the obstacles which hamper the struggling colony and independence is accomplished by armistice between belligerents, the first and natural excitement of passion having subsided and the honor between combatants being saved.

But this cannot be brought about, from the moment

there are dissensions in the colony itself, without the completest harmony within its bosom there would be a lack of that cohesion indispensable to lend strength and prestige to a new and independent nation, which has to confront, a unit, its compeers; without such perfect union, it would be manifest, that one portion of the community had been swayed by a caprice repulsive to the remaining portion, evidently convinced of the premature nature of the movement and hence the aim to be attained would carry within it the germ of abortion.

We wish to be fully understood in this matter. History presents to us cases in which a people has been subjugated by an alien race and the struggle of independence appears legitimate; union and harmony of purpose will not be lacking the nation which endeavors to expel the foreign invader. By common agreement the question of right will be superseded by that of local unanimity in the eyes of outsiders. We have witnessed this for a long time in Italy and we still see the example reenacted from time to time in Poland; the cause may then appear a just one, although not so by right, and universal respect will be granted the noble impulse which inspires the struggle against tyrannical and degrading oppression.

But, where no foreigners are to be expelled, where time and resources have been badly measured in order to snap the ties of a family compact, in which the elements are otherwise concordant, although opinions may differ, the case is an altogether different one. Even the vestiges of right, which may be appealed to to curtail the possession of the mother country in its own colonies on the basis of the simile of sons in relation to their fathers, alluded to in a former article, utterly fail to be applicable to the case and to have any force whatsoever, for there is not a whole colony in arms, but only a portion of one to the injury of both the loyal population and of the mother country.

It is hardly necessary to insist here on the extensive and powerful element of peninsular Spaniards, settled in Cuba. Some people call them strangers and even worse names. It will be necessary to remove all misconception on this important subject.

The name of *foreign interlopers* is altogether inapplicable to the Spaniards resident in Cuba and any body who has had occasion to study the population of the Island will have convinced himself, that, even the epithets of *ambulant countrymen* or men *temporarily* devoted to *industrial pursuits* could not well be applied to them without distorting the truth or common sense.

Have not native-born Cubans, as we have said on a previous occasion, been born the sons of Spanish fathers, who went to Cuba to work and who ere they made a fortune or after they had made it, large or small, have reared a family and live surrounded by it, and at the head of it, the very sons, who call them foreigners forming part of such family and all of them taken together being the only property owners which the privileged soil of Cuba counts?

In Mexico and the rest of Spanish-America at the time of declaring their independence the epithets above alluded to might not have been quite out of place, not however, in the mouths of those who most used them, but in the mouths of Indians, whose lands we had occupied and whom we had redeemed from barbarism, at the expense, of course, of their pitiable independence.

We shall go a step further and concede that much, that in those outlying provinces the sons of Spaniards declared their independence with a certain degree of authority, when it seemed to them better that to the duties they owed to their fathers, the liberation of the great majority of their native land should be preferred. The right to emancipation was in this case indisputable, because clearly founded on natural right; the question, there arising was not so much that of a son who prematurely strives to cut loose from his father, but of a whole people bent down by the force of arms or by a preponderating civilization to rules, to habits and to a government not any more congenial and, therefore, spurned.

But, in Cuba, where the only vestige that remains of the Indians is the record or natural history of their extinction, * where the whites are either Spaniards or their descendants, excepting always some families of foreign origin which have been intermingled with those of Spanish blood the epithet given to Peninsular Spaniards is devoid of sense, is the most extravagant aberration that can be put forward, coming

---

* We say the *natural history of their extinction* for the reason, that the Indians of the Antilles have not disappeared, as some believe and as Father Las Casas has written, by means of brutal hecatombs, of which there have been none, but by contact with a superior race, which by crossing the same went on producing other human beings more their image than that of the feeb'er aborigines. The same thing occurred in the Antilles from mixture between the white and black races, where it has been observed at the end of four or five generations as an extreme period, the distinguishing peculiarities and color of the negro disappear by the process of infusion of physical and moral superiority, brought about by our race.

from the lips as it does of the very men who would not exist and who would not have spread over the length and breadth of the Antilles but for the very qualities, those of an industrious people, which they fling into the faces of their fathers.

Why indeed should the idea of instability of residence be attached by some Cubans to Peninsular Spaniards among them? Has it not, on the contrary, been invariably the case, that all those Spaniards, who went to Cuba to work, when young, and who have piled up colossal fortunes there extant, have stayed and will stay, as long as they live, watching over the well-being of the families, which they raised in the Island while thus rising to wealth, preparing the brilliant prospects that await the unnatural sons who call foreigners their own fathers?

We should be wasting words, were we any further to dwell on this subject and we are, therefore, landed once more upon the fact, that that portion of Cuban population which strikes for immediate independence has no greater right than the remainder, which prefers staying within the folds of the mother country, developing the resources of the land, content to lead a provincial life instead of soaring in the elevated sphere of sovereignty with those indispensable conditions tacked upon it which constitute a rank so supreme.

Cuban independence should be solid, it should be founded on the united sympathies of all the elements of the country, there should be a deep conviction that perfect ability for self-government has been either reached or so very nearly so, that a little practice would suffice to for ever avoid the eternal political upheavings which have arisen in other emancipated communities, prematurely become independent.

It is only upon such conditions, that Cuba could attain independence and retain it without converting the delicate jewel into another Hayti or into a simple territory of the absorbing and little scrupulous American Confederation.

How then can independence be obtained and the mishap just alluded to be avoided? We shall in our ensuing articles endeavor to show.

## V.

**Important digression.**—Change of tactics by the leading promoters of Cuban independence in the United States and England.—*Autonomy*—Human *fallibility*. Impediments to the theory, and the force of logic.—Can Cuba be granted autonomy now?—That which we call autonomy—The real meaning of independence.—Spain's attitude towards both questions.—The advancement of Cuba in her political and administrative organization.—Its bearings as to the future—Why autonomy and not independence?—Hidden aims of this unexpected change of tactics.—Futile intrigue.—Damaging dilemma.

Whenever a work of the nature we have undertaken excites the interest, which the one in hand seems to attract among a numerous class of men whose clear comprehension is struck by it, the signs of the day, in as much as they may have a bearing upon the question, should not be unheeded. They will help to enlighten us all the quicker, that which we write down may assume the form of doctrine, if not sufficiently perfect as yet to settle the controversy from the very start (and we dare not aspire to as much), still complete enough to meet the innumerable points of principle and the weighty interests involved in a struggle, which we all wish should be ended. Thus the most unexpected, nay the most unlikely case has arisen which could have been dreamt of at the end of four years of armed rebellion to obtain an independence the feasibility of which we are searching for, and the case has been presented by the most determined and influential men within and outside of the Island that have been engaged in promoting the cause.

And we do not allude to an illusion, nor to a mere rumor. A new plan has been sketched out, although we are not aware, whether or not it has been duly weighed in proportion to the importance of the subject to be attained, and the plan takes out to Europe none less than Miguel Aldama, preceded by Fesser and Macias, accompanied by Aguilera and followed by José de Armas y Céspedes, the former irreconcilable opponent to any understanding, however reasonable and who has been the originator of the perilous leap which they have all undertaken.

*They go to solicit autonomy for Cuba*, the very men, who with tenacious resolution had pushed forward to proclaim her independence, in other words they go to prove in the face of the whole world that their attempt was a mistake after the lives of thousands of brave men have been sacrificed, immolated as they were, and the picture of desolation lit up by the glare of the incendiary torch.

We do not condemn this new step taken by the leaders, because of its differing from what they have hitherto pursued, error being the inheritance of our poor humanity, and to recognize and disown it is but proper, however late the acknowledgment may come. But we wish to have the change marked down as another proof of the fallibility of the human species and that our most irreconcilable opponents may take note, that in politics absolute truths need not be searched for, nor human beings that may not change their minds.

The sudden change which has been operated in the convictions of the individuals above named is, at all events, a most eloquent one, and we should not lose sight of it while we proceed, so that in their unshaken faith those who blindly revered them may not believe in the future.

Let us investigate, then, whether this new phase and the object it pursues are consonant with the interests of their native land.

To enjoy autonomy will presuppose the same capacity for self-government which would enable a nation to enjoy and practice independence.

Is Cuba ripe for autonomy? Can she govern herself and administer her affairs, with nothing to be added by Spain but her flag and name?

If this be the case, although the proposition may be excused, it is inacceptable as it stands. It cannot, on the one hand, suit Spain to be burdened with the experiment without the necessary authority to restrain and regulate; nor can it suffice the Cubans, who desire to move untrammelled, more because of its charm of novelty, than because they have duly weighed and calculated the matter, which they evidently have not. This mixed state of affairs could, indeed, hardly satisfy their ambition to its full measure, nor would it harbor the germ of durability.

Autonomy is a species of agreement between populations that would do as well, separated or united, without imperilling the interests of either or both. Such is the case between Great Britain and Canada, where the majority of the people are one, both by lineage and history, and where mutual interests are already so blended and consolidated, both morally and materially, that the form of government raises no apprehensions, nor even the question of independence.

In a case like this one, the mother country may grant autonomy without fear; it may, on the contrary, be even more advantageous to accede to it. Autonomy cannot be merely proclaimed. Time only will ripen it as a logical consequence of a series of natural reforms, which, by degrees, the measured development of populations will bring about.

This same development has been going on in Cuba. History is there to prove to those who will impartially, and without distorting it, examine into what has taken place—that the administration of Cuba has been vastly improved during the last quarter of a century the furthest.

There were no elective "ayuntamientos" twenty-five years ago; law-courts were not then independent, as they are now, from civil authority; there was no local legislation—everything under this head radiating from a centre, the absolute arbiter of all initiative; the process of law was not administered as it is at the present day; there was no council of administration, with the attributes of a consultative body, flanking superior authority, as is now the case.

All these reforms, sketched out in a few words, were carried out in Cuba within a lapse of time which could hardly have been shortened to meet the case, and with such practical results, that the municipal sphere was doubled; and even important provincial experiments were made with reference to the three headquarters of subdivision in the Island.

The favorable consequences of gradual development in colonies clearly shine forth from what we have said, so that they may, in due course of time, be fitted for self-government. This has recently been accomplished in Canada after two centuries of a well regulated vitality, and the same would have been the case with Cuba in due time, for within a century of progressive advancement, she has reached colossal proportions therein already.

But supposing the time of self-government had arrived for Cuba, autonomy, or independence, would be indifferent, like in the case of Canada. According to the belief of the leaders above named, the time has arrived, for during the past four years they sustained this conviction by word, by the sword, by their action, and by their money. Why, then, should they, who but yesterday strove to be independent, cast about for autonomy, the one case calling for as much capacity as the other?

The movement is positive; none of their agents ignore it. EL CRONISTA discovered it a week ago, and *La Revolucion* did not deny it. Does the movement represent the unanimous sentiment of all seditious Cubans? Why, then, if this be the case, do they go on crying in the Is and, and repeating it in their newspapers, *long live independent Cuba?* Is the "autonomy movement" merely the action of a few? If this be the case, who warrants the submission of the bulk of the insurgents?

It may be a mere artifice and snare to the Spanish government, for the fall months are the most adapted to the sending of reinforcements to the army in Cuba. If this be the case, they certainly have ill-judged our men in power.

Or do they act in good faith? If this be the case, they are lacking in logic; they are traitors to the sentiments of their fellow-believers who want Cuba to be free, and not autonomic.

We could pin still further important considerations upon the same subject did we wish to lengthen discussion; but we shall let the matter rest, and merely sum up in the following words: Either Cuba possesses the ability and elements of self-government—and, in that event, she may be independent—or she lacks them, and to ask for autonomy would be an absurdity, or else treason.

## VI.

Taking up again the thread of the pending treatise with two alternatives of article III.—Between preserving and destroying the prosperity of Cuba on becoming independent such as now situated, the latter alternative is the most likely to occur.—Attention of the Cuban emigrants to this the is.—.Proof.—Why and when the United States might take possession of independent Cuba.—Statistics of population of the Island.—Dissolution by diversity of race.—By nationalities.—By political parties.—By numerical disproportion of sexes.—The natural consequences of these unfailing developments in hampering the consolidation of independent Cuba.

With two hypothetical queries as an alternative we left pending in article III of this treatise the scientific solution of the question we are investigating. The one laid down the problem of the conservation of independent Cuba in her present condition, and the other of her natural dissolution by the heterogeneous character peculiar to the elements there extant.

We do not deny, that between the two phases, we, for our part, saw more clearly the second although the first one were more agreeable to us, and that we rather dwell upon this one, and as this tendency of our mind will not be accepted by many without further explanations and as furthermore we cannot allow ideas of similar importance.to drift along at random, while going to the bottom of this question, we shall argue to-day, supported by the statistics of Cuba, so as to enable us to demonstrate certain ideas, which have been uttered, in as much as this may be feasible. Our aim shall be to let the most rigid truth rule our attempt to discover a solution for this question by dint of sincerity and pains-taking.

It is always a difficult task to arrive at the objective

point of an undertaking having for its aim civilization and magnanimity, while individual interests and the impatience of inexperienced masses, discordant in sentiment, have to be reconciled and considered. We may say, on this occasion, however, and not without pride, our opponents have paused, that they have flung aside their usual blindness and thus do honor to their intelligence, for they are reading EL CRONISTA with the attention, which the subject in hand demands, nor has as yet a single voice been raised to interrupt our argumentation.

When this can be said of a body of men, much good may be expected of them. Those, therefore, who at a great distance read these lines, need not think that the emigrated Cubans do not peruse them, and that by not noticing what we say, pretended toleration is exhibited, for in this city alone upwards of three hundred of them pay enough attention to it to come in quest of the paper and from all parts of the Union we daily receive letters asking for the complete series of issues beginning with the first one in which the treatment of this important question has come to be inaugurated.

Leaving at rest, then, these first signs, eloquent as they are and reflecting credit as they do, we have still to add, that their importance increases by the very character of our arguments, which can hardly fail to strike the most superficial reader. Men of less intelligence, and particularly men of less toleration would have ceased to bestow any attention upon what we are writing. We are glad to observe, therefore, that the contrary is the case, a circumstance equally creditable to that class of our readers and to EL CRONISTA; to them, because the truth is beaming forth upon them and they perceive it, and to us because they doubt no more our sincerity.

It is nothing but due to remark that EL CRONISTA is not only the acknowledged organ of the Spanish race in America, but that it is also the most active and complete commercial medium, which for a long time has been published, semi-weekly, at New York, in the Spanish language.

In article III, we intimated, without saying so in as many words, that it is evident, that if Cuba were to become independent to-day, there would be no homogeneous blending of the masses, that there would be no order and no cohesion among political parties; the very reverse of what we perceive, where the common welfare rests on a solid basis, and where the common interests are well developed already. Nor would independence now obtained solve in Cuba the labor question and yet leave unshaken the wealth there accumulated, a wealth, which lends to the Island the great importance it possesses, nor would there be anything to invite the indispensable immigration; foreign capital would take good care not to run the gauntlet of a gradual deadlock, that would irremediably paralyze mercantile transactions there with the sudden decrease of production to which the colonial staples raised in Cuba would be liable.

On the contrary, as an immediate consequence of emancipation the heterogeneous elements would be decomposed, now held side by side in groups in that rich country, sheltered as they are beneath our national flag. This decomposition would arise from the very rancor of a bloody struggle of four years, recklessness would dictate disorganizing and imprudent measures, where science and philanthropy should preside. In a word, the spectre of race would all of sudden stand erect across the fair Antilles, and with it the danger of a common Haytian Republic, which, towards the East would stretch all the way to St. Thomas, and would take in Cape San Antonio towards the West, calling upon the American people to step in and interfere. Such interference by the United States would have for its motive merely strategical reasons, for there would be nothing left to invite commerce and industry; the interference would not be for purposes of annexation, the practical and sensible people of the Union would care very little indeed, to acquire a country promising to be a dead load only.

It should be remembered in dwelling upon the dread prospects here conjured up were Cuba to become suddenly independent, that the Island now counts a population of one million and four hundred thousand souls, about seven hundred thousand of whom are of African origin, and that in their sentiments upon the question of race the latter are in perfect unison. Now, as for the remaining half, the white population, the same includes 70,000 Peninsular Spaniards, 49,000 Canary Islanders, 50 natives of the Philippines, 500 Porto Ricans, 2,600 Frenchmen, 1,240 Englishmen, 500 Italians, 450 Germans, 150 Portuguese and 100 other Europeans, 2,500 Americans, 3,420 Spanish-Americans, 150 natives of Yucatan, 32,234 Coolies, 64 Dominicans and 25 Brazilians.

It will thus be seen that there are 170,000 whites, not born in Cuba, and that there would thus remain, to confront the 700,000 colored people, 530,000 creoles, held to be all white, but were we to examine more closely, even among them subdivison would be necessary.

The white population of the districts, where rebellion has reared its head against Spain, including Sancti Spiritus and the Villas already pacified, amounts to 307,359 persons; as 36,384 of them are either Peninsular Spaniards, however, or foreigners, the native population is shown to be 270,975 only, in all the districts, which have been in insurrection.

It would be just as much of an absurdity to suppose, that a rebellious spirit animated all these inhabitants, the majority and the best from among whom have been and are still fighting the insurgents by the side of the Spanish troops, as it would be to consider loyal all the people, natives of the Island, who live in the remaining districts, where peace has not been disturbed, a great many from among whom have fled the country, while others, who have not done so, conspire against Spain in the dark.

Setting then the loyal at heart, belonging to the present and past rebellious districts, against the rebels in undisturbed ones, we may assume as pretty much beyond doubt and cavil, that the number of white creole inhabitants, who would prefer to cease being Spanish subjects, amounts to but 270,000.

We do not pretend to say that this would be the number of Cubans, that would remain in the Island, were the latter to gain independence under prevailing circumstances, dangerous as such independence would be, considering the large number of colored people and the spirit which animates them; but the most barefaced will not deny, that so far as Peninsular Spaniards are concerned, at least one-half of them, now side by side with us, would prefer to quit the country, on the one hand, because they would not like to be exposed to the hatred of those who are their bitterest enemies to-day, nor on the other care to stand the brunt of convulsions, which the fearful question of races would sooner or later explode beneath their feet.

Another problem here arises as regards the relations between the white and colored inhabitants, that would remain in the Island.

The white population is pretty nearly equally divided between the two sexes, while among the colored people there are two men to every female. Consider then, that most of the Peninsular, Canarian and foreign inhabitants are men, and we have the fact before us, that the white element that were left in Cuba suddenly made independent at the present moment, would prove to be physically by far the weakest.

In order to narrow down the computation, we will assume that 500,000 men of color remain, including the Indians from Yucatan, the Chinese coolies and the dregs of foreigners, and it will be granted, that the adherence of such an element to the new Republic would be anything but a boon.

Conceding further, that among those, who remained in the Island, the sexes were equally divided, we shall yet be brought back to the fact, that white men would stand in the proportion of one to every three men of color, and that in the newly created position in which the colored population would move, physically strong as it is, the very independence of Cuba would be threatened, scarcely acquired though it were, and that its consolidation would be an impossibility.

It will thus be seen, that the question as it is constituted, is such a complicated one, that in all its phases of life it has so many ramifications in whichever direction we may undertake to analyze it, that even upon the most superficial search we stumble upon the fact, that those, who have undertaken to stir it up in arms, have but indifferently considered its manifold bearings. We, therefore, beseech our readers, to go on following our investigation with the same leniency, they have hitherto shown us, and if then, on terminating the study, they yet persevere in believing, that we are in the wrong and that its solution should rather stand committed to the arbitrament of the sword, we shall wash our hands in innocence, if Cuban independence never be reached, while on the other hand it may be attained, the natural tendency of colonies, remote from the mother country, being towards independence, as we shall by degrees point out in our work.

## VII.

Why the question of race would explode at once beneath the feet of independent Cuba.—Eloquent examples.—Character of the negroes under control.—Character of the negroes when left to themselves.—Brutal excesses committed by them in parts of the country in insurrection.—Many from among the Cubans in insurrection would as little wish the Island to be ruled by negroes, as by Americans.

The dread prophecy that a war of races would convulse Cuba, were she to become independent such as now constituted, has not been thrown out in either a flippant or arbitrary manner. The same thing happened in the French portion of Santo Domingo even before internal affairs had been profoundly disturbed, for the negroes availed of the general conflagration in which France found herself wrapped up all of a sudden. A subdued struggle for mastery is even now going on in the Southern States of the American Union, although the phenomenon is at present manifesting itself somewhat differently.

The struggle for supremacy between one subdivision and another of the great groups which make up the population of a country constituted upon the latest model, has nothing unnatural in it, and we witness it constantly in communities, whose elements are a little discordant, especially where they are so by the difference of race, or by that of religion and finally by politics as to the best form of government.

The catastrophe, which a couple of years ago bent down France, had essentially its origin in nothing but the difference of race.

How frequently has not Belgium been converted into a field of Agramante by the question of religion, as to which should be the predominant one, staining with blood the pavement of its beautiful capital, and carrying the strife to the very halls of Parliament?

And look at Spain herself, where a standing contention is going on between two systems of government for the past sixty four years, so much so, that the adherents of one form or another would very nearly appear ready to sacrifice the very national existence upon the altar of their idols, did not the proud character which distinguishes our country screen her forever against every plan of disintegration?

The question of supremacy in a country, shaped upon the spirit of our age, is bound up with its very life, for the traits of its character thus will it.

Transfer, then, the question of supremacy to Cuba without the means of repression. Picture unto yourselves a state of equality and liberty as radical as independent Cuba would entail it, and consider that the black population would be three or five times superior in numbers to the whites, and then let the most enlightened, the cleverest and the most energetic from among our enemies declare, what means they would employ to keep within bounds the natural aspirations of a powerful and vigorous majority, which, from the threshold of popular conventions to the extremes of material preponderance, would have at command not only its own followers as a body, but the government of the country itself.

Can there be imagined a more childish conception, than the illusion which those have been indulging in, that dreamt of angelic harmony in the new commonwealth, the object of their ambition, a state of affairs, from which the awakening would be a blood stained reality! And there are men who do believe that all that were necessary would be to shout: "*Viva Cuba independiente*" from the Morro of the Havana and independence would be an undisputed fact stripped of peril!

The negroes, it cannot be denied, have given proof of docility and submission to the white supremacy on the Island, so much so that the almost incredible instance has occurred of a single overseer, with four or five white subordinates, having sufficed to hold undisturbed sway over from two to three hundred colored men.

But this has been owing to, and will always be contingent on the more immediate surroundings, on the strength of the government and the state in which the country chances to be. Do our misguided adversaries think otherwise? Were not Hayti and the general massacre of the white inhabitants there as a warning at the time of proclaiming the independence of the French portion of Santo Domingo, we should but have to point at the atrocities committed by people of color in insurrectionary districts, of which women and children in particular have been the victims, and this has been the case notwithstanding the fact that they were under rebel military discipline, and that they knew that Spain still held under sway the Island. And news of these atrocities did not merely come to our hearing with the usual exaggerations, which distance from the scene of action is apt to superadd, we have been able to ascertain the truth about them; we have been near the scene itself, and the heartrending cries of victims have filled our breast with horror. The author of these lines has lived in Cuba many years; has visited the various departments; has had access to the archives; has travelled over the length and breadth of the land; has lived on the sugar plantations, and finally served as a soldier during the insurrection so that he might personally learn the truth.

A split between the two races would be inevitable from the very commencement, and soon degenerate into open hostilities. But even were this not to take place at the very start, does not the struggle now going on originate from a secular divergence between Peninsulars and Islanders, ridiculous and puerile though it may be, who on looking closely into the matter we find to bear towards each other the relation of fathers and their sons. How long do our adversaries suppose the example would remain without followers among the colored population, when similar scenes of rebellion would be re-enacted, ending in upsetting the authority of the whites themselves, and in finally exterminating them.

But, aside from a general massacre, or something akin to it, two alternatives thrust themselves upon our consideration: the one the spread of the Haytian Republic all the way towards the Cuban west end, Cape San Antonio, and the other the superseding action of the United States alluded to on a former occasion.

It is self-evident, such as the matter stands, that Cuba would not gain its independence, such as Cubans desire it to be, and as united Spain desires that in due course of time it should be attained. Our task having for its object to point out how independence may eventually be reached, we shall throw all the light procurable upon the investigation of the case in hand in subsequent articles.

## VIII.

Mistaken notions about the real interests of the United States in connection with Cuba.—Speculative character of the American people.—Is dualism in harmony with the opposing conditions to which it subordinates itself?—Contrary results, which this circumstance of itself carries along between professed sympathy and real action.—The dualism as it affects Cuba, to the disappointment of those who counted upon action.—Why Cuba in the hands of Spain is most acceptable to the United States.—Economical proofs, drawn from commercial statistics in the United States.—What the incorporation of Cuba in the American Union would entail.—Examples drawn from the history of other Islands of the kind in various conditions, and from Mexico.—Advisableness to cast aside prevailing prejudices and attempt the solution of similar questions by the light of Science.—The discredit attaching to forcible possession and disastrous consequences to the conquering nation.—The absurdity of *manifest destiny.*—The exceptional case that would urge the annexation of Cuba by the United States.

Those who suppose the United States have any immediate and positive interest in taking Cuba, are very much mistaken, nor are those less so who believe that the selfsame motives which now prevent the consummation of any similar scheme while we have the Island would still keep them in check were Cuba independent to-morrow, unless circumstances there subsisting were at the time radically changed.

There are two striking features in the American mind producing a dualism inexplicable to the superficial observer. The one is the practical spirit which guides the Americans in everything to be accomplished, and the other created by their constitution and by their unbounded material resources, filling the popular masses with the belief that there are no barriers which can be interposed between their ambition and its attainment.

It thus happens that frequently both the government and the press put forth the most absurd ideas and conflicting with the very facts they are aiming to bring about; not that they are ignorant of the very extravagance of such ideas and the political, social or economical drawback which would be inseparable from their accomplishment, but because they know the national character which they guide and portray, an l which they do not care to curb, fully aware as they are that finally the law will have to decide and that in conformity therewith harmonious action will then be reached.

These being the leading traits of the American character, it is not easy for those to form a correct judgment who but superficially watch and study its manifestations; and in the Cuban question, above all others, words and action have been so widely apart that frequently people have been intimidated by suspicious tendencies, by sympathies and antipathies, to which greater importance has been attached than they in reality warranted, inasmuch as the practical mind of the people in the end would subordinate and control manifestations of the kind and place a question of such nature within manageable shape.

We have, in fact, but to cast a glance at the annual fiscal statements emanating from Washington and we shall find the figures to be of a nature to prove, that from whatsoever side we may search them, they carry convincing proof that it suits the United States that Spain should have Cuba as long as she is able to keep possession of the Island, and this is the real secret of the conduct of the American government in handling the various questions that have arisen while events took their course.

The total imports and exports into and from the United States in their commercial intercourse with Spanish America and the Brazils for the fiscal year ending June, 1870, amounted to no less than one hundred and ninety one million dollars.

Cuban trade contributed thereto 71 millions, Porto Rico 11, or be it 82 for the Spanish Antilles; follow the Brazils with 31, Mexico with 19, the tropical British-American possessions with 15, the River Plate Republics with 12, Colombia with 10, Chili and Perú with 9, Hayti and St. Domingo with 4, Venezuela with 3, St. Croix and St. Thomas with 2, and Central America with 2, the remainder being made up by the French Islands and Cayenne.

On superficially examining these figures, people will be led to suppose that the material riches of Cuba would, if anything, kindle the wish in the United States to possess the Island outright; but when we come to consider that the peculiar nature of the labor question is tied up with this very abund nce of wealth, and that wherever bl ck labor has been disturbed, it has alw ys, to a vast extent, become unproductive at once, and that sl very woul l disappear with the act of incorporation, the immediate consequence wou'd be the curtailing by one half of Ameri an trade with tropic l America for the mere p'easure of plac ing a dead load upon the shoulders of the United Sta es, while, on the other hand, the good sense of the Ame ican people, under the influence of its most solid int r sts, is bound to prevent the consummation of any such un l.r- taking, preferring, as it naturally will do, that Cuba be retained by Spain.

This conservative course has a much wider bearing upon commerce than the mere figure of eighty-two mi li ns through the ramific tions of labor and dealings to which they lead, productive of sustenance to the people at large, and in government circles this is also fully understood, for sugar and tobac o being the main staples of import from the Spanish Antilles and producing a la ge revenue, some fifty or sixty millions of duties now collected thereon would be wiped out at once, since at least from Cuba, on her in. corporation, these artic es would enter duty free.

That Cuba would be unproductive, or nearly so. from the moment she ceases to form part of the S anish dominions, can be easily shown, not by pointing at the figures above detailed, which, for the rem ining c untrie , are small in comparison to the extent of territory of the majority of them, but by keeping before our eyes the example given by St. Domingo and Jamaica, whose elem nts of labor when emancipate l, and whose vicinity afford most suitable comparison.

In 1790, St. Domingo exported of colonial produce $27,828,000. In 1870 the trade of the Island with the United States amounted, as shown above, between imports and exports, to but $4,000,000, divided between the two Republics, without counting, it is true, what European trade may have been at the time. And this at a time, when the Island had long emerged from the more immediate consequences of the terrible catastrophe.

But, leaving aside this Island for the very reason that the catastrophe was brought about by a war of races, and supposing that in Cuba an upheaval of this kind were never to occur, let us examine into Jamaican events and the teaching they convey, there having been no independence in this case, but merely a disorganization of labor.

Movable and immovable property was upon the eve of

emancipation represented in Jamaica by £50,000,000, while in 1850 its value had declined to a little over £11,000,000; five years after emancipation labor had been stopped on 605 valuable plantations; and its population has in the meantime been as steadily decreasing, as that of Cuba has been increasing. We could, indeed, hardly add any more convincing proofs, even were we to go on expatiating upon the subject.

What then shall we say with respect to Mexico? While being the largest Spanish-American Republic, with its independence acquired half a century ago, its population of more than eight million inhabitants, a rich, fertile and extensive territory, that country appears with an amount of trade comparatively small as compared to Cuba, in its business with the United States, its most natural market.

It is evident from what precedes, that Cuba, made independent ere she were ripe to be so, or labor there were thoroughly transformed by a measured process, would but add another example to the many already given all over Spanish-America. It is furthermore clear, that it does not by any means suit the United States that such risk should be incurred, since it would be tantamount to killing the hen that lays the golden eggs.

Now our century chances to be preeminently a utilitarian one and the useful side of a question is not left unheeded. Masses, it is true may yet be swayed by the charm of glory, and although in the United States the abstract idea of glory would not of itself suffice, masses may yet be carried away by tendencies to expand dominion, like some are wont to attach to the Monroe Doctrine, yet the American people is above all a practical nation and prefers undertakings of greater usefulness, and whenever a solution is to be found for any given question, the one which does not destroy its commerce, will meet with greater favor in its consideration. The American people imperturbably follows its own course, although it may not at once openly disavow the utterings of sentiments more or less tinged with the artificial and hence of passing effect. The imprecations of those who find themselves checkmated in their chimerical plans will be listened to with as much forbearance, as good sense in its application to the true interests of the people at large will have a tacit support.

Besides, the expeditions of boundless conquest narrated by history have been a good deal discredited by its teachings. At the time, when to overgrown Rome, the world seemed to be getting too small, the horses of Attila stamped their hoof marks on the altars of her Gods, and when the sun had ceased to set upon the vast expanse of Spanish dominion, she came very near being parcelled out between some European nations.

Into the word manifest *destiny* (el destino manifiesto), so often unconsciously repeated by the masses, we need simply to drop an *a*, to make it manifest nonsense (desatino manifiesto); for can there be anything more absurd imagined, than the pretension to carry out throughout the *republican part of our hemisphere* the useless strife of the three emblems of war, that were carried about in imperial triumphal processions on the old continent.

Very differently the case would present itself, however, were the United States compelled to interfere by reason of endangered interests within the Mexican Gulf, whether such imperilment arose from some dread disaster, a state of anarchical dissolution or of complete exhaustion. There would, in such an event, be no commerce left, or very little of it, to cause the Americans to hesitate, and Cuba would be merely annexed as a territory.

Is this perchance the degrading prospect which the Cubans would wish their country!

But let us drop the subject. this article as it is, will do.

## IX.

Previous propositions are not absolute on the ground of individual interest.—Other phase of the question.—Exigencies of the personal policy of the American President, leaving to another artificial party the responsibility of a disastrous war.—Cuba's mission regarding Spanish-America.—Strange conduct of a portion of the latter in the Cuban question.—How the Antilles may become towards the American Continent that which England is to the European.—Cuba merged in the United States would be a constant threat to the Spanish-American Republics.—Different features of supremacy and dominion of one people over another.—The immolation of Spanish-America a foregone conclusion with the insurrectionary Cubans, who appeal to American intervention against Spain.—A ruinous end easily avoided.

On endeavoring to show in our previous article how unwelcome to the great mercantile interests of the United States the separation of Cuba would be, either to be annexed to the Union, or to be left independent, we omitted to mention, that some statesman or other may take it into his head to make capital, by fostering among the masses the idea of forcibly depriving Spain of the Island.

We all know but too well the human heart to understand that ambition or cupidity have but too great a sway over it, nor should we allow ourselves to be lulled into a fancied security regarding the question in hand; for are there not cases in which a President might be tempted to sacrifice the interests of the Republic to his personal ambition and foster a war cry for electioneering purposes?

History is filled with examples of this kind, not only where constituencies are to be influenced, but where a man in power is already well and firmly seated, if therefore in the midst of a presidential campaign one of the candidates flattered the instincts of the masses by conjuring up the prospects of an extension of territory, in order to capture votes, it would not at all be surprising, were a question of this nature put forward, ruinous though it proved in the end to the country that stirred it up.

Professional politicians in Republics above everything else usually look to their own interests first and to those of the people at large afterwards, and provided public opinion can be swayed through the instrumentality of pretended patriotism and heroism and all the clap-trap of an ensnaring phantasmagoria, so that personal interests may be secured, the consequences are often little heeded and there are besides plenty of means to transfer the load of responsibility to other shoulders and put forward other grounds of action wholly distinct from the original one.

The question here touched upon is, therefore, very different from the preceding one, and we shall analyze it as such. As we have repeatedly said in EL CRONISTA, Cuba presents a peculiar case, in as much as she will be both directly and indirectly accountable for any action of her own towards the rest of Spanish-America, that consequently she dare not proceed in the most vital question without the greatest circumspection, for one false step may entail imminent peril to the remaining Spanish-American populations, and that, the spell once broken, it will be impossible to master further dangers in the future.

It would be difficult, indeed, to determine what may happen to Spanish-America, were Cuba incorporated in the United States. It is but too evident to the eyes of all of us, that sympathies more or less spontaneous, are given to the ill-begotten insurrection, an insurrection which would end in the annexation of the Island to the United States, if successful at the present day. Sympathies of this nature, lacking in logic as they do, are with difficulty explained, except we try to find their origin in that meddling spirit, which, in the midst of undoubted and visible progress, characterizes the XIX century.

Cuba, the key to the Mexican Gulf, the natural stepping stone towards the isthmus, the link between the Southern and the Northern portion of the New World, Cuba, the Queen of the Caribbean Sea and the most valuable jewel from among the islands that stretch out towards the Ocean, harbors within her many attractions of material wealth to ambitious people, as well as a strategical position of the first class, from whence the whole Continent may be dominated.

A respectable power, whose dominion nobody would dare to encroach upon, could be reared, were these in themselves magnificent gifts properly availed of in conjunction with the remaining Antilles, her sisters, that may raise themselves to a level with her by degrees, while Cuba may rise to that of Porto Rico, an Island that has very nearly reached the age of manhood already. Such a power would be as safe from encroachment, as England is in her position towards the continent, in which homage is done her, and in which she is both feared and admired.

But an independent nation cannot be called into existence from one day to another in the Island of Cuba sufficiently strong to make front against all dangers, both internal and external, and as the Cubans would not like to run the risk of being superseded by the blacks singlehanded, the inevitable fate would be that of a territory of the Union first, and next a State.

Let us ask, then, what guaranties would there be left for the independence of the remaining Republics being preserved, from the moment that the absolute sway of the Gulf of Mexico fell to the lot of the United States, carrying along that of the Isthmus as the natural consequence? Where would Mexico remain; where Venezuela? And alluding but to the ports of Aspinwall and Panamá, what of them? What guaranties should we have for the transit by canal through the Isthmus, now projected, should the absorbing Anglo-Saxon race claim absolute possession at that point of interoceanic traffic? Dominion does not merely spread by conquest and the sword, it also makes itself felt by insolent dictation at the hands of a powerful neighbor, all the more galling, as we may have nothing to oppose to it, and the more exacting, the more we bow to it.

Are we to understand, that Cuba is ready before-hand to lay on the shrine of a hasty independence her own individuality and that of all Latin America to boot? Yet, there are men to be found in Latin America who sympathize with an aberration of this kind!

There are insurrectional Cubans who would not shrink from committing the suicide, though as fully convinced as we ourselves that what we say would be inevitable; they would willingly sacrifice both Cuba and the rest of Spanish America for the doubtful boon of not remaining the sons of their fathers, for to cut loose from Spain precisely conveys this meaning as the matter stands.

Can there be anything more hair-brained, while the paths that naturally lead to the independence of a nation are so easily travelled, and of a nation, too, that not only may remain the absolute mistress of her own destinies, but a natural buckler to her sisters!

# X.

Further concessions.—The case of independent Cuba without black domination or American absorption.—A foretaste of public order and material welfare.—What foreign investors would do, now residents of the Island.—Precedents and conclusions.—Present Cuban dissension a foretaste of future quarrels.—The influence of business paralyzation.—The a sets and liabilities of independent Cuba.—Politico-economical comparisons.—The army,—The navy.—Standing requirements.—Inevitable dilemma; none but a powerfully constituted Cuba can fulfill the destinies, to which she is called by nature.—Her first untrammelled movements after independence should remove all apprehensions on that score.—Her break-down as an independent nation would entail the position of vassalage of Latin America towards the United States.—Historical proofs.—The filibustering of a Walker.—Why it failed.—Summing up and deductions.

Our readers shall not have occasion to say, that for the sake of upholding exclusive opinions, we shall deny them the possibility of Cuban independence without improving the present condition of affairs there, without transforming and increasing the population, without keeping labor well organized, and without preserving the wealth of the country. We shall go further, even, and concede that the Island may consolidate a new state of affairs like the rest of Spanish America despite great material drawbacks created by independence, despite the danger inseparable from the colored element, and notwithstanding the no less perilous disposition to acquire new countries which may be lurking in the American mind.

The horizon of possible eventualities stretches out over an expanse so vast that whatever the human mind may choose to grasp, may be comprised in it. This, together with the circumstance that our searches in this matter are eminently philosophical, inasmuch as we strive to draw the light of truth from the darkness of ignorance and error, and place it before the world, obliges us to meet our opponents upon their own ground, and there to ventilate the question judiciously.

A philosopher once said that the mould of our poor humanity is slippery and of so ethereal a consistency that you dare not breathe a word of contradiction without breaking and destroying it by the fit of indignation into which it is thrown.

This being the case, and our own experience having during many years confirmed to us the truth of the simile, it is clear that we should commit a great mistake were we to proudly and intolerantly decline entertaining any hypothesis from the opposite camp except such as evidently led to a well-determined solution within the precints of our own opinions.

Although we have every reason to believe that if Cuba obtained independence to-day, she would be unable to re tain it on account of the respective character of the races that would form the nucleus of the population, and on account of the schemes that would arise with respect to the Island in the United States, we shall grant that Divine Providence, by special favor, may so dispense her blessings that the negroes would abstain from disputing supremacy to the new society and the Americans from extending their dominion over it.

There are circumstances in the life of nations, however, which radically change the direction into which their action would otherwise expand, and the two alternatives we have placed before our readers could thus, nevertheless, occur without partaking of the miraculous.

Let us, then, concede that, by a stroke of good luck, Cuba become independent in the condition in which she now finds herself situated, and, furthermore, that she consolidate her new state the same as the rest of Spanish America.

But while thus consolidating her political status, it by no means ensues that her material prosperity will be placed on as firm a footing. It would be expecting a great deal of her, indeed, were we to suppose that such could be the case, inasmuch as prosperity there is bound up with the quality of labor at her disposal, incompatible, as the same would be in the estimation of every sane man, with the constitution that would rule independent Cuba, limited as the financial resources would at the same time be. Cuba would require twice as many financial resources as she possesses to be able to have the same rank as the Island now occupies, or she would have to stoop down to the position of a country whose independence was merely tolerated; not that she were to derive any material benefit from such exalted position, but to prevent being sneered at the same as Hayti and other similarly situated countries now are. Good sense and discretion would, above everything else, be expected of Cuba in the handling of her policy when lifted to the rank of an independent nation, and this so practically and visibly shown, that none of the foreigners she would then comprise in her population may take it into their heads to upset the state of affairs existing.

This would be all the more requisite since for a lately subsisting system of labor, a new one would have to be substituted in the midst of a sudden diminution of production, and at a time when foreign industry and capital could only be retained among them were their interests fully protected.

Let us ask, now, by way of parenthesis, whether the most prominent leaders of the insurrection have given sufficient proof of their capacity, or inspired confidence, at least, that they would understand how to successfully bridge over matters at a juncture so precarious in directing the power of state craft?

We, on the contrary, perceive them to be split up in personal fractions, kept together by an ephemerial and adolescent power, which, as yet, offers to them no greater enjoyment than that of satisfying their vanity. The foretaste of the future of their Republic thus held out, is such, that we are involuntarily carried to the conclusion that the country would like St. Domingo or Venezuela be handed over to interminable factions, even granting them that much that the catastrophe of Hayti were not repeated.

But casting aside these considerations, let us follow up the thread of our treatise, showing the expenditure that would be involved in carrying on the existence of the new nation so that such existence may be useful to itself and the outside world, and we see arise before our eyes the installation and maintenance of the whole fabric of the new power, with its executive, its chambers, its diplomatic corps, its consular officials, its administration through all the branches clinging thereto, its army, the national militia, and above all the navy, for being an Island situated at the most important point in all the New World, it is clear, that either the new Republic must be the owner of a powerful fleet, or will have to relinquish holding that position, which both, self-respect and necessity, would demand for the country's own sake and that of all Spanish-America.

In 1866 the budget of the Island for ordinary expenditure amounted to $26,852,673 or be it about twenty seven millions. Part of this, we will admit, would be saved by independent Cuba, but what would be the difference if any between the cost of sustaining independent and Spanish Cuba?

Granting even, and we grant much in admitting it, that our administration of the Island, be expensive as it is and that the Republic would have to cut down expenses in various branches, the saving there effected would be swallowed up by the necessity of upholding its sovereign state within and without, and we do not believe that we exaggerate when we calculate, that the expenditure would aggregate at least twice as much as the amount above indicated.

In the army perhaps a great saving might be effected and the $8,000,000 set against that item in our budget might be cut down to half as much; but the recruitment, cost of armament, the replacement of forces would on the other hand have to be added, and in the end it would appear, that if any difference there be in favor of the new order of things in this item, it would prove altogether insignificant.

There next follows in said budget the navy with $4,000,000 and with this item quite a different feature is here looming up, for Spain would not leave behind her navy, and Cuba, for the reasons given, could not dispense with one.

Consider, then, the cost of creating and entertaining a navy, and it will be conceded that from whatever point of view you look at or approach the question of this all-important element, independent Cuba will have to expend from $50,000,000 to $60,000,000 annually for carrying on the normal life of a Republic, or cease being a nation worthy of the Spanish descent and of the position which Providence has singled out in her favor.

To begin with, the income of the new nation would have to be doubled. And, how can this be effected from the moment that its incipient life by a new labor system curtails its large productive powers? On the contrary, the bare fact of Cuban independence would reduce its income by one-half at the least, and hence all the elements which are now to be found there under our rule, instead of being preserved, would vanish together with the prestige, which now surrounds the Island, however much its new masters might be endeavoring to prevent it.

The consequence then and there arising would be deplorable indeed. Cuba would be carrying on a life fluctuating between feebleness and mishap by reason of incapacity, the same life which the St. Domingo and Venezuela of to-day are dragging along, and towering above her and the rest of the Spanish-American family there would be the supremacy of the American Union, without the respect in which that supremacy is held at present by the flag that floats over Cuba.

Can the readers of EL CRONISTA entertain any doubts on the subject? Remember but the piratical expeditions of Walker to Central America, both of which placed in imminent peril the liberty of those populations, but as Spain had something to lose in Cuba, the third expedition was thwarted from Europe, and Honduras had the honors of the fourth one.

Summing up, then, we repeat that Cuba might be independent to-day, and remain so, if by mere chance it so happened that she were not converted into a second Hayti at once or that the United States did not absorb her, but a greater miracle would have to happen, were she capable of carrying out and persevering in the task without serious detriment to herself and the remainder of Spanish-America.

And, since Cuba may attain independence with a more promising future before her, with a providential mission to fulfill for the common good of the Spanish race, does not the damage which our opponents do their own country smite their conscience, when they come to consider that they can do it so much good for a future not remote? We shall more fully explain in another article.

# XI.

From the proofs given, and that which has actually taken place, the veritable origin of our opinions has arisen.—Proofs.—The military condition of Cuba at the beginning of the insurrection.—Spain's confidence in the loyalty of the Island.—The conspirators all the more active.—Territorial subdivisions of the Island.—The loyal portion.—The disloyal one.—Population of the one and the other compared.—Comparisons and summing up.—The true state of public opinion in the Island.

The arguments, which we have been engaged in adducing, are, within themselves, so solid, tending to prove as they do, that Cuban independence, such as the Island is at present situated, would either carry along the most deplorable downfall ever occurred in any nation whatever, whether Cuba become the prey of horrid negro sway, or whether she be gobbled up by the Americans, or whether the whites succeeded in governing her like they do the two Republics nearest to Cuba, similarly situated as they are in point of climate, soil and population, that we have but to cast a glance at statistics on the one hand, and at history on the other, in order to give strength to what we are putting forth. We shall not, in doing so, merely cling to casual events, which may have been more or less an emanation of the spirit that animates the people of the Island, but shall on the contrary go on, proofs in hand, with proofs indeed, of a less controvertible nature, such in fact as human science can produce, and besides, the opinions which we give, are not those of EL CRONISTA, they are but a pale reflex of the most general and respectable opinion, which has ever been and is still uppermost in Cuba; and that it may not be said that this is an arbitrary assertion and that it would be difficult for us to prove it, we shall dedicate this article to procuring such proof, and, important as the subject is, shall use statistics on the one hand, and actual occurrences on the other. Spain little dreamt of what would happen in Cuba; the small contingent of soldiers in the Island at the breaking out of the rebellion will go far enough to show this. On the contrary, the home treasury had been borrowing money from the Bank of Havana; the amount was a large one, having been swallowed up by the Dominican and Mexican expeditions, and the intention of the government at Madrid was to cancel this indebtedness by making economies under the head of the army, the heaviest and least productive item at the time in Cuba.

Hence, the usual reinforcements to the army in Cuba had for a long time ceased, and instead of keeping there the ordinary force of about 25,000 men, there were barely 12,000 on the spot, when the luckless movement at Yara startled the Spanish government into measuring the grave mistake made.

Not a soldier was to be encountered in the purely rural country between Point Maysí and Cape San Antonio, nor were there at the various district headquarters sufficient forces to reach even approximately half their ordinary complement.

The Island being an extensive one and a great many military posts having to be attended to, the fortified places fared little better than district headquarters did, and neither of them had half the garrison to make front against a rising.

Hence, the Yara rising thus took everybody by surprise, and the insurgents, marching upon Bayamo, captured the place, the insurrection thence spreading further in mind and deed without any serious check.

While Spain was placing full confidence in the loyalty of the whole Island, events have proved, and the proofs are multiplying, that even several years previous to the breaking out of the rebellion, the disloyal Cubans had been concerting matters, and had been getting ready for the struggle. In their own pamphlets they have solemnly declared, subsequently, that such was the case.

We should keep well before us, consequently, the arrangements made on the one hand, and the march of events on the other, in order to fully understand the general drift of what happened. Had the greater portion of the creoles wished to be rid of Spanish dominion, as we are every day told by the insurgents, the thing might then have been accomplished without Spain having the time to prevent it.

After settling this point, let us; by the help of statistics, examine of what the elements consisted, for, unless logic has ceased to be logic, the proofs we shall bring forth will lead us to a just appreciation of the real sentiment there prevailing.

The Island was then divided into three departments and into thirty-two jurisdictions. The one department is the "Oriental," starting from the imaginary point of Gibara to Manzanillo, traversing Holguin and the Tunas, and in the east terminating at Baracoa. The next is the "Central," reaching from the same imaginary line across towards the west, by traversing the Camagüey, and ending at the Cinco Villas; and the third is the old department of the west, or "Occidental," covering the rest of the Island all the way to the Vuelta Abajo.

The rising at Yara, as we have intimated before, communicated itself at once to the Oriental department, with the important exceptions of the various district headquarters, where the Spanish flag was left floating, and whither all the many Spaniards withdrew from the surrounding country. The movement subsequently spread to the Camagüey, from whence it obtained a vigorous support, leaving the cities of Puerto Principe and Nuevitas on our side, while a couple of months later the insurrection also reared its head in the mountains of the Cinco Villas, although faintly and in small numbers.

It should be here added, that the insurgents have made the very greatest efforts to bring about the revolt of the Vuelta-Abajo, but the Spanish nationality has in the hearts of its sons been deeply engraved, and whosoever from among the faction undertook to try his luck in this quarter did so not only to the loss of his illusions, but of his life besides, from impulses of loyalty in men, their brothers in blood and origin.

A flood of light will here be thrown upon the subject, when we come to consider on the one hand the populations of the rebel districts, and on the other, those remaining true to the faith of their fatherland and family. We shall draw the line in a manner that will not leave room for cavil, and add such modifications as the strictest impartiality may call for. We remarked that the Oriental department unhesitatingly supported the rising at Yara. It is important, therefore, to examine the population returns of each, which were: for Baracoa 10,800, Bayamo 31,336, Santiago de Cuba 91,351, Guantánamo 19,421, Holguin 52,123, Jignaní 17,572, Manzanillo 26,493, and Tunas 6,823. The total for eight jurisdictions thus sums up 255,919 souls.

Out of the Central department we can call in full revolt at the time but two jurisdictions, those of Puerto Principe and Nuevitas; for in the remaining portion, from Moron to the extreme west end of the Villas, the rebellion was born of elements so very slim, that pacification has already taken place, and even at the time that the revolt was in full swing, it shrank from attempts to sally forth from the roughest mountains, which there attain extraordinary proportions.

In the census, the taking of which preceded the Yara affair, Puerto Principe appears with 62,527 inhabitants, and Nuevitas with 6,376, or be it 68,903 all told between the two, and adding their number to the above enumeration, we have an aggregate figure of 324,822 inhabitants.

It should, in justice, be observed that the positive fact is here brought to our notice, that a body of country people, inhabiting the Villas, took share in the movement, and fairness towards our antagonists requires that we should take them into account, and we shall even go as far as to give them credit for one-half of the whole population of six additional jurisdictions, inclusive of Sagua, as devoted to their cause. Be it known, then, that Cienfuegos counted 54,034 souls, Remedios 47,247, Sagua la Grande 51,986, Santa Clara 52,644, Saucti Spiritus 45,707, and Trinidad 37,509, making up a total of 469 384 souls.

But on the other hand, the striking fact should not be overlooked, that the headquarters of the territory under arms, with the sole exception of Bayamo, took sides with Spain in the struggle. This is easily explained by the fact, that there clustered around them the most distinguished individuals, enlightened, and having most to lose. Not without a good many individual exceptions, however, in this case, in which the persons were frivolous and dissipated young men, but it is not necessary to take them into account, for, as a set-off, we have the Spaniards in the country whom we did not count in the above enumeration. Deduct, then, from the grand total the inhabitants at headquarters: Baracoa 2,364, Cuba 36,491, Guantánamo 1,735, Holguin 4,954. Jiguaní 1,347, Manzanillo 5,643, Tunas 1,840, Nuevitas 2,208, and Puerto Principe 30,585, or be it altogether 87,167, and we discover that the extreme figure of population, on which the insurgents based their operations, did not exceed 382,217, even with all the liberal allowances we have made.

Now for the contrast which is presented by the loyal portion! Here we have the following population: at Bahia-Honda 12,773, at Bejucal 23,748, Cárdenas 50,465, Colon 64,217, Guanabacoa 26,213, Guanajay 39,843, Güines 62,462, Havana 190,332, Jaruco 37,571, Matánzas 79,462, Pinar del Rio 68,926, San Antonio 33,886, San Cristóbal 28,977, Santa María del Rosario 8,046, Santiago de las Vegas 15,850, and the Isle of Pines 2,087, showing that in the districts alone, where the insurrection was unable to take a foothold, there are 745,289 souls. Adding thereto the 144,561, being one-half of the population of the Villas and Sagua and furthermore the 87,167 eliminated from the other headquarters, and we arrive at the fact that the people, inhabitants of the Island, not wanting to be independent, are summed up in the grand total of 977,018 souls, against 382,217, seemingly all of a contrary opinion at the breaking out of the insurrection.

A good many men abroad have at once given their sympathies to the insurgent cause, carried away by a generous impulse imparted by the representations of emigrated Cubans, who spread the impression that the troubles in the Island have their real foundation in a split between Cuba and Spain. Such representations they have implicitly attached faith to without examining more closely into the matter. These sympathizers will do well to study the statistics we have just given in these columns in order to be convinced that there is no such question pending between Cuba and Spain, that on the contrary, the said troubles have sprung from an insignificant and thoughtless minority, localized, as it is, which has risen against the majority that surrounds it, and against their country.

Even at the risk of tiring our readers by entering into further details, not the less important in their bearings upon the question, and hence indispensable in lending force to our argument, we shall take up again the thread of argumentation embodied in this article in the succeeding one.

## XII.

New proofs.—The disloyal population of Cuba is not only the smallest in number, but also the poorest.—Proofs.—Territorial division of the Island into sections.—Lands under cultivation.—Uncultivated lands.—Richness of the soil occupied by the loyalists.—Compared to that in rebel districts.—Relative and positive proportion between the two.—The loyalty of the largest and most valuable part of the Island is thus unquestionably secured.

The work we have undertaken would not fulfill its purpose, if we did not follow up gathering proofs, as we have already been doing in the preceding article, proofs intended to absolutely and indisputably show, that the Island of Cuba does not now aspire to sever its connection with Spain, that but a small minority is bent upon such separation, which tries to force its will upon the Island and the entire nation by persistently adhering to such scandalous undertaking, and we, therefore, go on producing and completing the documentary vouchers, which are to lead us to an unimpairable demonstration. Let us then take up the thread of statistical analysis, the scientific test and touchstone by which the progress or decline of nations is measured.

We said, and have furnished ample proof, that something like three-quarters of the people of Cuba are of one mind with us; as it might chance, however, without partaking of the miraculous, that these three-quarters failed to be the most important and the richest portion of the community, the smallest being at times the best representative body, we trust, that we shall not tax overmuch the patience of our readers in trying to show, that in this case the very reverse is observable, for, not only is the population of the rebel districts the numerically smallest, but by far the poorer. Let us then establish this fact in an incontrovertible manner by applying to it the same method of calculation adopted in the foregoing article.

The totality of "caballerías" of land comprised within the Oriental department, by adding thereto Puerto Príncipe and Nuevitas, which by way of expediency we shall put down as having risen in a body, amounts to 272,741. We certainly proceed far in thus including Santiago de Cuba, Guantánamo and Baracoa, which, we are all aware, are not in rebellion. The Villas, by adding thereto, Sagua, show an aggregate of 190,036 "caballerías," and in taking one-half of the latter and adding the same to the jurisdictions in insurrection, the area, that could be assumed as having risen in support of the already much circumscribed movement, would cover 367,759 "caballerías."

Our adversaries can hardly fail to admit, that we make liberal allowance as regards the extent of territory, for we grant them more than half of the entire Island, which contains 629,886 "caballerías."

But this very item, even assuming it to be true, would operate against the aspirations of our antagonists. Wishing to be more than fair in our arguments, we have accepted the item as a fact, although in reality it is not. But from the moment we push the search a little further, we shall discover, that while conceding them so vast an extent of territory, the relative wealth of it is considerably less important.

Out of the 367,759 "caballerías," over which the insurgents were wont to roam at the time of the rebellion reaching its culminating point, there are but 16,809 under cultivation of produce of all kinds, and as the sum total under culture in the Island amounts to 54,102, there will be found to be 37,293 in the loyal territory.

It should, here be added, that out of the 16,809 "caballerías" of improved lands in rebel hands, 4,200 belong to the half of the territory under culture near Sagua and the Villas, and that these cultivated lands have never been in possession of the insurgents, the districts having besides been pacified since.

Due note should be taken of this circumstance, for from it we arrive at the conclusion, that the jurisdictions, where the Yara movement took root, are restricted to those of the "Oriente" with Puerto Príncipe and Nuevitas, whose total area of 272,741 "caballerías," only embraces under culture of all kinds of productions 12,609, or be it barely five per cent.

And, furthermore, eliminating the Villas and Sagua from the jurisdictions in which the rebellion has never been able to get a proper foothold but to bring to greater relief the loyalty of its industrious inhabitants, the striking fact is presented of 33,092 "caballerias" (out of 166,999) under cultivation. The remarkable proportion of about twenty per cent. of cultivated land is thus shown to be embraced in the jurisdictions loyal to Spain.

The foregoing would of itself suffice to demonstrate and furnish the analysis of respective importance as between rebel and loyal jurisdictions, did we not apprehend that somebody may not accept the same as conclusive testimony, and that he will raise the question, as to whether a less extent of area under cultivation may not in reality be proved to be richer by the nature of its products, than the more extensively improved one.

Such is indeed frequently the case elsewhere, and might be supposed to be the case in Cuba also.

Some people always make it a point to lift their own crotchets above the heads of all, however clear the case under discussion may be; since we, however, have striven to leave nothing of what we bring forward without a solid foundation to rest on, we shall now produce the last proof necessary for the diffusion and establishment of a redeeming idea, a proof which renders nugatory from the very commencement the objection previously alluded to as not unlikely to be raised.

Now, it chances to be, that the most valuable productions of the Island are sugar in the first place, and next rum, molasses, honey, bees-wax, coffee and tobacco, the remainder, with the exception of mahogany and cedar, do not, properly speaking, constitute articles of commerce, used, as they more exclusively are, for local consumption and trade only, such as the cereals, meat, vegetables, fruit, &c.

Out of the articles of colonial produce we have named, there accrue to the districts we have conceded to be contaminated by rebellion, the following: 6,197,783 arrobas of sugar, from light colored to brown, five-sixths being of the latter, Muscovado, and but one-twelfth white; 27,971 casks rum; 41,138 casks of molasses; 305,085 barrels of honey; 30,377 arrobas of wax; 445,439 arrobas of coffee, and 226,371 mule loads of tobacco.

As shown by official statistics, the distribution among the loyal portion of the Island, is the following: 36,422,-876 arrobas of sugar, only 13,000,000 being Muscovado, and more than 16,000,000 box sugar; 96,162 casks of rum; 340,357 casks of molasses; 269,653 barrels honey; 38,043 arrobas wax; 296,103 arrobas coffee, and 129,209 mule-loads of tobacco.

In drawing a comparison between the two, we find that the loyal districts produce six times as much sugar as the rebel ones, and that in point of quality of the leading article of produce in the Island, the same proportion of at least a six-fo'd superiority characterizes the loyal part.

In rum, we have a three-fold larger production in the loyal part, and six times the production of molasses and honey taken together, and without drawing a line between the value of the two liquids. Wax shows a quarter more in favor of the loyal part, the latter producing two-fifths less of coffee, and nearly one-half less of tobacco also.

As regards the latter two articles, we have to make some remarks. The coffee plantations of Guantánamo have by themselves clung to the Spanish cause, with very few exceptions, and the tobacco produced in the Vuelta Abajo, in the Spanish districts, is worth, as a general thing, from five to six times as much as that which used to be raised in the Vuelta-Arriba, in rebel jurisdictions. By reducing to dollars and cents the two articles, the difference will be found to incline from three to four times on our side.

From the preceding, we therefore arrive at the following conclusion: If, on the one hand, the population of loyal districts stands in the proportion of three souls to one versus the supposed territory of the rebels, wealth in the loyal side ranks six to one, on comparing the loyal portion of the Island to the rebel districts. And, on going into details, in order to discover the cause of this extraordinary disproportion, the best test is presented to us in the most renowned of the rebel districts, the *Camaguey*, which has been called *the richest and most civilized "par excellence"* by amplifiers on the side of our enemies. While covering an extent of territory of 82,409 "caballerias," and thus being the largest on the Island, we find there but 1,318 under cultivation; under artificial pasturage there are 5,478, wild meadows embrace 37,960, and the balance consists of dark forests, of wild cliffs, and of impenetrable underwood, which the footsteps of man had left undisturbed until the rebels converted the region into a rabbit-warren for the purposes of loop-holes of refuge.

And it should at this remarkable juncture be mentioned, by way of parenthesis, that this very circumstance affords us a clue to the protracted defence in a part of the country where it would long ago have been overcome but for the impenetrable fastnesses covering it.

That the Cuban insurrection wears, by no means, a general popular character, the notes we have given in the previous article will long ago have convinced the most exacting reader, and he will be anxious, therefore, to be led on to the main thesis of our proofs. We shall, consequently, take in hand this principal sub!ect in the next following article, and thus conform to their wishes, without losing sight, at the same time, of what has thus far been proved.

## XIII.

Fresh considerations.—The men of the insurrection.—The usual biding places of leaders.—Cárlos Manuel de Céspedes.—Francisco V. Aguilera.—The Figueredos.—Peralta.—The Quesadas.—The Agramontes.—The Agüeros.—The Arangos and their diverging views of the question.—The Varonas.—Sanguilí.—The Cavadas, the Villegas, Jesus del Sol, Villaamil.—Arredondo and his catastrophe.—Goicouria, his antecedents, his movements and end.

Other important considerations are crowding upon our mind, which should be embraced in this work, emanating as they do from previous reasoning, in order to prove, that Cuba has not risen in arms against Spain and that she is not even bent upon a premature independence, which would forthwith work her ruin in either of the forms we have insinuated. That which we are bringing forward is not our own opinion alone, it is that of the bulk of the Cuban people, with few and incompetent exceptions. And that which we now propose to dissect is neither intended to show the manner, nor the proper moment, how and when Cuba may become independent, although we finally shall point out all this, but it is to establish this very circumstance of prevalent sentiment in the Island.

The subject we have taken in hand is so paramount in importance, it is so blended with and of such a powerful influence upon the main thesis, from which it takes source, that even did we succeed in convincing the most refractory minds by the light of truth through this work of ours, the question as to unanimity of sentiment in favor of independence would be constantly recurred to, although such unanimity does not exist. The impression of its existence has been artificially infiltered into the minds of civilized nations in general, and it is imperative, consequently, to get at the truth upon this very suqject, so as to prevent its being availed of against us Spaniards.

While striving to carry out this aim of ours, we are again compelled to resort to a digression, which cannot fail to spread light, and is, therefore, both indispensable and urgent. An intimate interest attaches to the subject of this digression and though independent of the basis of our arguments, it may prove of prime importance in determining that which we wish to get at.

In thus fulfilling our duty in a straightforward manner and not with motives which malice might attribute to it, we have to combine proofs arisen from previous articles, and pass in review the most distinguished leaders of the insurrection, in order to prove, that the element here exhibited was not composed of foreigners to the soil of Cuba, but one native-born. It will go to show the part which the remaining population played and enable us to destroy other suppositions, as well as unjust accusations, which till now have successfully put afloat by some of our detractors.

We have here, foremost of all, the celebrated Cárlos Manuel Céspedes, a lawyer of Bayamo, whose scientific acquirements we shall not now discuss, nor even the condition of his economical interests, which some say were not of the most brilliant at the time of the rising at Yara. All we want, is to point out the place from where Mr. Cárlos Manuel Céspedes hailed, so as to show that this individual has no connection with the districts that have staid true in Cuba to the mother country of their ancestors.

The same has reference to Francisco V. Aguilera, to him who styles himself the Vice-President of the Cuban Republic with the greatest formality, for although the descendant of an illustrious branch of Spaniards, long identified with the Island, himself and all his many relatives were born in the districts, where the insurrection originated, and they were all, most of the time there living and doing business.

The Figueredos, also, from the Oriental department, have always, according to the more or less important positions filled by them moved within the territory assigned in this work to the rebels, content in not transferring their activity to a wider range in cooperation with others in every respect their superiors.

Aside from these three names, we do not remember any one worth mentioning in the wide expanse from Yara to

Baracoa, unless we also point out Peralta, who was from Holguin, and unless from the crowd others may be produced, even of less importance than this one.

From the Orientel department to the vast pasturage of 80,000 "caballerías" of uncultivated land called the *rich and civilized Camaguey*, there is but one step and we shall let imagination take us thither and review the leaders that were there marshalling the dissident forces.

Quesada was the first, and in deference to the serious character of our labors, we shall not call him the heroic, nor shall we search for reasons which carried him into the camp of the insurgents, for he was a fugitive from justice for an ordinary infraction of a bad nature. He is a native of Puerto Principe, the same as his brother, who also figures as a secondary leader, although they are both far removed from the theatre of hostilities. This and their birth go to show that they had nothing in common with the Spanish districts, and if not questionable, their faith in the cause of independent Cuba is of so rare a quality, that we are in doubt as to its being made up of opinion or from a sentiment of personal responsibility for the infraction alluded to in the one case.

We let Agramonte follow Quesada, with all the subaltern derivations of name and family that either actively or passsively sided with the rebellion, some from among whom have returned to the Spanish side disappointed and repentant on account of the absurdity of their aspirations, while others have perished in the struggle or have gone for good to a foreign land.

The Agueros are also of relative importance to this luckless insurrection which has pushed Cuba upon the brink of an abyss, from which her own sons have snatched and are snatching her. But the Agueros are also from Camaguey, the same as the Quesadas and Agramontes, so that that their revolt also fails to convince us that they are the representatives of premature Cuban independence on the part of any district on the Island staying on the Spanish side.

The Arangos have also taken an active part in the rising of their locality, although never insp·red by the same idea as the rest; and as a good many were carried away by their example in the Camaguey, another important consideration here presents itself, and that is, that there was a great difference of opinion observable there, to such an extent, that we Spaniards might well claim at least one-half of the population, the Arangos never pretending to the independence of the Island, but only to obtaining liberal concessions, more or less numerous and more or less opportune, within the folds of the country of their fathers.

From the immense and thinly populated part of the Island another noble name gave the insurrection its contingent. We mean the Varona family, some young members of which, leading an adventurous and profligate life, also joined the insurgents, more for the purpose of escaping a life of privation to which they had been reduced in the United States, than for the good of their country.

The general saying is that they were brave in their revolt, although much might be lessened under that head; but, brave or not, they on the first occasion withdrew from the theatre of events, and this goes to prove that besides not being natives of the loyal districts, their faith in the practicability of the cause they had embraced is not an unshaken one.

How could we otherwise be able to explain that others stay there, arms in hand, who are deemed less valian', while the Varonas have been travelling abroad, the one honorably following up the scientific career taught him in Spanish universities, while the other makes the best of ridiculous actions, supported by the liberality of some fools?

But it would lead us astray, were we to cite other persons from the districts alluded to, unless we take into account the beardless Sanguili, a thoughtless cadet who has been seduced into deserting from Havana to join the insurgents, and who attained a certain degree of celebrity for having had the bad luck of being crippled during the first encounter by a Spanish bullet.

Next come the Villas, stretching towards the western extreme, where the insurgents succeeded in roaming about during two years, and in this locality the Cavadas, the Villegas, the unfortunate Jesus del Sol, and the still more unfortunate Villaamil, are the only names that have been heard there as leaders. These were all born in the same districts that witnessed their discomfiture, except Villaamil, who was a native of the other side, all furnishing us additional proof of the unanimity of sentiment that has been all along existing in the more prominent districts, as has been shown moreover in the article preceding the last one.

If we are not mistaken, Arredondo was a native of Havana; nothing very particular was known respecting his name till he became seduced by the erroneous belief which misleads a good many, that even the air in Cuba breathes revolt, and invaded the Vuelta-Abajo in order to cause a rising in the locality, the expedition proving so disastrous, that not one of those who participated in it remained to tell the tale of it, the lesson being given by natives of the Island themselves.

From the sphere of prominent men, the shadow of but one rises to protest against our thesis, that of the unfortunate Goicuria, who made to the Camaguey the last trip of his eventful life in a manner very nearly constrained, and who might pass for a representative of the capital of the Island, inasmuch as he was a native of it. For aught we know, he may have been born in Matanzas instead.

But what did Goicuria represent in the aspirations of free Cuba? A remini-cence of annexation plans cherished in the days of López and Crittenden, when the slave States of the Federal Union wanted to gather new forces. The same thing which Macias represents, not upon the theatre of the struggle, although he calls himself a colonel, but through the noise made by English newspapers. Many from among these would not as willingly lend themselves to his lucubrations if this circumstance were shown to them, or if he did not so well pay for the publication of the nonsense he over and over again writes against Spain.

Goicuria—may he rest in peace, we do not wish to cast blame upon him—had never been back to Cuba, nor was he well informed of the spirit that animates the Island, except by misrepresentations of an interested and absurd nature. He went there a representative, to say a great deal, of his own personal antecedents, and more under compulsion than of his own free choice, for the prestige of his former actions. We say thát much in order to remove any argument not to the point, and shall wind up this important digression with our next article.

## XIV.

Local occurrences in their bearings upon the personal inclinations of the lower classes that joined the insurgents.—New proofs of total disagreement between individuals from the loyal and insurrectional districts.—Incendiarism and its character during the struggle.—Its significance in weighing and analyzing public opinion.—Its decisive results in favor of Spain.—The military forces of Spanish-Cubans against independent Cuba.—The volunteers.—Their numerical strength.—Statistics showing Peninsular and Insular volunteers.—Partial facts relating to the Matanzas district.—Difficulties in drawing a precise line between the two camps and definitively clearing up this point.—Prominent character of the Cuban chiefs of the volunteer militia.—Prominent character of creoles commanding troops of the army.—Contrast with what took place in Mexico.—With what happened in South America.—Deductions.—Character of our opinion.

In the same strain in which we have expressed ourselves with respect to the extemporaneous and highflying movement of the leaders of independent Cuba, we might proceed and speak of the smaller lights of the insurrection in general, supported by more numerous facts, for although at its height it had a brigade called that of the Vuelta Abajo, the number of its adherents was so limited, that it did no good, and finally was dissolved.

It is advisable, that explanations of this kind should be made at this juncture, so as to enable us to more fully master the question; for although it is nothing but natural, that the masses should not have rushed forward in sufficient number to lend the rebellion a local complexion while the leading men of the richest and most civilized jurisdictions of these territories failed to respond to the call of the thoughtless movement, some blind enthusiasts might still labor under the impression, that strategical reasons caused the theatre of the strife to be confined to jurisdictions without culture, as presenting the greater advantages.

But all suppositions bearing upon these points have to be shorn of their plausibility by referring to the general order recommending the application of the torch and waste-laying, which the so-called President of the so-called Cuban Republic issued, so that the apathetic might be stirred up to join its banner and Spain deprived of all resources in Cuba.

Were the Island in revolt to the very air it breathes, as some tenacious spirits will continue insisting, is the case, the crazy proclamation we have alluded to, would have sufficed at the time to set ablaze this overcharged atmosphere, and to prove that the phrase was appropriate to the occasion. What better opportunity, indeed, could have been afforded to patriotic enthusiasm to set fire to the roof of self and neighbour, involving in common ruin the enemy, and thus parodying, by carrying out the command, the heroes of Saguntum through the extravagant imitation of the fugitives of Bayamo.

But, with irresistible eloquence facts at once came to render patent the real state of affairs. The richest, the most populous and most civilized jurisdictions of the Island despised the command and not only made a common front of loyalty for the country of their noble kinsmen, but hurried forth, enthusiastic and ready for the fray, swelling the ranks of the volunteers, and sending the men by the thousand into camp to side with us.

Nobody can deny or gainsay these facts, for the solemn and truly glorious proceeding of the brave batallions of Guines is well-known, as well as that of the warlike firemen of Havana, of the Cuban-Spanish counter-guerillas, who took permanently active service from the Villas to the extreme east of Baracoa, and of all the remaining citizen forces, who have cooperated with such resolution in support of the banner of Spain in the Island of Cuba.

Some may think, that we go on writing as the fancy strikes us in favor of the object we have in view, without continuing to back up with facts and documents that which we pretend to affirm, but as EL CRONISTA is determined not to produce anything at random, but to adhere to the mathematical arsenal of statistics, which admits of no shifting artifices, we shall now furnish that which we have ascertained upon the subject, of the greatest importance as it is.

There are in the Island, 58,293 male Peninsulars, and putting down one-half for boys and old men, including those otherwise unfit to bear arms, and assuming, as we well may do, that the remaining half is incorporated in the corps of volunteers, or be it 29,642 Spaniards born on the other side of the Ocean, there still remain 30,000 native Cubans making up the upwards of 60,000 volunteers.

We have another book at hand offering still more conclusive evidence and going to furnish the most irrefutable proof. We allude to the partial statistics of the various volunteer batallions of the Matanzas district, one of the points in the Island, where Peninsular population has more thickly settled, in which we find registered with their full names and places of birth, 5,933 men within the jurisdiction, including 710 native-born Cubans.

From this argument, although it rather diminishes the general estimate which we wish to arrive at, the following dilemma arises, which cannot be demonstrated away: either there are in Cuba at least 60,000 volunteers, as every day we are told by our adversaries, to increase the importance of their faction, and if this be the case, it cannot but be confessed that half of them are Cuban creoles, or these mischievous volunteers are all Peninsular-Spaniards stifling in Cuba the patriot sentiment which breathes in the very air. From what precedes it is rendered manifest, that not one-half the number of *interloping Spaniards*, whom, the *innumerable emigrants* declare to be under arms in the Island against them, are thus enrolled.

It would fortunately be an easy task, were we to undertake furnishing the names of those who would affirm the first case of the dilemma, for in Havana alone, we know a good many leaders that hail from that city; among others of no less prestige and renown, the marquis of Aguas Claras, Calderon, Ampudia, Olano, and Sotolongo, a list that we could extend considerably from memory.

And once that we have taken in hand this subject, another most eloquent proof should be availed of, forming a remarkable contrast with what has happened in other parts of Spanish America on their ceasing to do the bidding of our country.

We allude to the brave creole captains of the Spanish army, who have had the privilege of taking part in que'ling this mischievous rising that uselessly disturbs the Is'and of Cuba for the sake of some ambitious men.

General Ferrer, Brigadiers Ampudia and Acosta y Alviar; the Colonel of Sappers Villalon; Lieutenant Colonels Santelices and Garcia; commanders Pérez, Michelena, Don Manuel Herrera Dávila, and a good many others that we could name but for memory failing us, and the list proving interminable—all living witnesses to the unpopularity, the ill-timed nature, and moral and material discreditableness of the movement which they confront.

In Mexico, for instance, and in all the Spanish-American countries which precipitated themselves into the strugg e for independence during the first third of the century, the commanders and officers of the Spanish army, natives of the soil, took a different course, and this should be noted down, without our wishing to offer any apology for the line of conduct thus adopted.

Thus Allende, Aldama and Abasolo were captains of the Queen's regiment; Iturbide wore the badge of a brigadier ere he assumed the imperial ermine after the "plan de Jguala," and Don Antonio López de Santa Anna had obtained from the King of Spain a similar dignity, or was at least a colonel in the army at the time of his enlisting on the side of patriot independence.

Shall we go still further and add, in order to convince our readers on the Spanish Main, the names of other leading chiefs that stand prominent on the records of their history? For there are Bolívar, Mosquera, Castilla, and others of no less repute, that issued forth from the ranks of the Spanish army and confronted their old and brave c mrades in the same sense, as we have shown to have been the case in Mexico.

What do we, on the contrary, witness in Cuba, where the very atmosphere is declared to be impregnated with revolt? We do find men precisely situated as were those above enumerated, fighting side by side with us during the four years' strife that has been going on.

Let us pass that which we have said and abundantly proved, viz.: that nothing of a general national sentiment can be discovered in Cuba, except the one in favor of Spain; we find that Cuba is Spanish, if we eliminate from the population an insignificant and disowned minority, and that the opinions which "EL CRONISTA" is emitting in this ungrateful task are *not those of* "EL CRONISTA," *but of Cuba herself.*

## XV.

The majority in Cuba is ruled by conviction and not by expediency.—Marvellous progress of the Island during the past ninety years.—The increase of population in Cuba compared with the increase in the United States.—Territorial extent.—Positive contrasts.—Favorable consequences as regards prosperity in Cuba.—More comparisons.—Cuba and Porto Rico in reference to St. Domingo and Jamaica.—Foreign residents in Cuba.—Their position towards the question endorses Spain's management of her colonies.—Other contrasts and facts.—Cuban wealth compared to American.—Estimates of extent of territory, population and wealth between the two.—The present condition of St. Domingo and Jamaica denies the assertion, that the Spanish Antilles are exceptionally constituted—

Nor could this be otherwise, unless a fit of universal insanity caught hold of the public mind in the Island, and since some malevolent censors are constantly declaiming against the moral and material backwardness in which they allege Spain keeps the Island entrapped, this is also debatable ground, upon which we are bound to cast a ray of truth, so that the injustice of this slander be seen and that another reason may be rendered patent to show the abundance of motive which impels the great majority of Cubans, as well as the most enlightened and wealthy from among them, to be on our side while the struggle be proceeding.

There is no nation, under the heel and oppression of tyranny, as some pretend to say, Spain keeps Cuba, that progresses in the shape and to the extent that she has been doing during the past ninety years. What we put forward in venturing to say that much is positive. The climate of the Island is of a nature, that one-third of its average immigration is doomed to succumb to it and this circumstance lends additional force to the statistics we shall produce in order to place beyond a doubt that which we have just asserted.

At the time that the United States consummated their independence, they counted about 4,000,000 inhabitants and Cuba no more than 170,000, while in 1862, the one had a population of 31,000,000 and the other of 1,400,000, thus showing, that while the former country had during this lapse of time multiplied the number of souls in the country by seven and three-quarters, we had done so by eight and a quarter, the greater gain being in a surprising manner on our side!

It should be here remembered that in the United States the increase of population not only arcs> from the normal progression of a country teeming with abundance, moral in its habits and virtuous in social intercourse, as this country was during the first fifty years of its independent life, but that the daily accession of population by European immigration on a vast scale, added to great acquisition of territory, contributed towards its reaching such fabulous figures, that the thirteen States came to be thirty-seven since, each of them occupied by bonafide settlers.

In point of immigration, and acquisition of territory Cuba has of course no parallels to exhibit in comparing the one country with the other. The Island was under the influence of the measured tread of civilization and of a labor peculiar and natural to her, and has, therefore, not been able to expand in a like manner under this head. And since tyranny, wherever exercised, does not carry its impulsive force far enough to oblige the sexes to propagate the species as the Holy Writ commands, the inference is that the population of Cuba must have been in comfortable circumstances, indeed, in order, even to outdo in the increase of population the United States, that the prosperity there must have been very different from what our defamers would make people believe and from what oppressive and tyrannical sway would lead us to suppose.

Prosperity in the Island is proved by another fact revealed from statistical search. Starting from the favorable influences which the climate and fertility of soil bring about to stimulate reproduction of the species in tropical countries in general and in the Antilles in particular, we have an exception presented in the case of St. Domingo and Jamaica, both possessing the same advantages of soil and climate and yet declining in population in an alarming manner, instead of increasing.

The fact then, about to be brought to light, is of a decisive bearing upon the question having reference to the 11,200 foreigners, that were settled in the Island, when the revolt at Yara broke out, in as much as they stay in the Island, happy and content to do so; 6,601, or more than half their number having been born on this side of the Ocean and among these 3,633 natives of the Spanish-American Republics.

This group of foreigners is a living protest against the false imputations as regards the government of the Island, for why should the freest men on earth come and settle in a country, systematically oppressed, in numbers quite respectable?

Wherever a government is oppressive, the very reverse takes place, the natives emigrate in great numbers, such as we observe in the case of the Irish exodus and their removal to this country. Now, it so chances, that emigration from Cuba on an extensive scale has only been started by the Yara revolt.

Another item that should have our immediate attention is the fabulous wealth of the Island compared with that of the American Confederation. The very best barometer of the prosperity of a country is the wealth of its inhabitants, and this wealth on the other hand is dependent upon the inherent nature of its administration; with the excellence or drawbacks entailed by the latter, the accumulation of riches will, in the long run, either rise o decline.

Cuba produced in 1862 the value of $305 919,875. The United States showed an accumulation of wealth in the same year of $24,448,663,172; and calculating the production thereon at the rate of 7 per cent., for we have not at hand the precise figures, this would show $1,711,406,422, or not quite six times the Cuban production.

The United States had at the time twenty-two times the population of our Island, and eighty-six times the extent of territory. It is shown, therefore, that the comparison greatly speaks in our favor, each individual producing $55 in this country against $218 in Cuba.

The concentration of riches and productiveness here exhibited in the case of Cuba is so great, that it would hardly be fair to dwell upon the vast extent of territory from whence the American Union draws its annual quota of the world's production.

Will anybody dare to deny that the local administration has a paramount bearing upon the production of results so surprising, and that any other government would insure them as well? Search, then, into the cases of St. Domingo and Jamaica, in natural resources the compeers of Cuba, and Porto Rico, and if the comparison be not a pertinent one—although we cannot see why it should not—take up the case of St. Domingo and see what the Spanish part of the Island was under the sway of the Castilian crown, and what it is now as an independent and sovereign Republic!

But the life of a nation is not bound up with its material riches alone. Intellectual life has its value, too; and on this very point Spain is misrepresented in her endeavors by those who would fain tear away from her her vast possessions.

We shall postpone the investigation of this subject to another article.

# XVI.

Another phase.—The intellectual progress of Cuba on a level with and even superior to her prosperity.—The historial character of Spain with respect to the important subject of her colonial system. – The University of Havana.—The programmes of study.—The superior institute of humanitarian studies subordinary to the University.—The professors of both schools and the superior and local juntas of public instruction.—Instruction in the Island nearly exclusively monopolized by Cubans.—Brilliant results which deny the assertion, that there has not been a sufficiency of scope for intellectual advancement—Personal examples.—Eloquent comparisons between civilization and instruction. —Professional and preparatory schools for all careers.—The state of Cuban instruction compared to that of the generality of Spanish-America.

Public instruction is the first sign of spiritual life in a nation. A country may passess boundless wealth, nature may shower upon her spontaneously grown material resources of every imaginable kind; but this cannot be said of Cuba, for the real wealth of the Island consists of the labor bestowed there on nature's gifts. While abounding in innumerable resources, a country may be lacking refinement and civilization to such an extent, that the material and intellectual power may there appear as far opposed to each other as the two poles.

An example is offered to us by California at the time, when the gold mines were yielding countless riches. The most adventurous Americans were there collected together, and among them the roughest, and many grew prodigiously rich; but life was of a precarious tenure and justice and the law were dealt out practically and brutally, a half-barbarian retribution called "lynch-law" was resorted to, setting at defiance public morals and advancement.

It then, no doubt can be entertained, that the most favored of the Antilles, aside from its extraordinary prosperity, is equal in intellectual culture to any one of the countries on the American continent, is it not evident that the mind has its sway there in due proportion to its civilization and character, that the reproaches made to Spain are malicious and abusive, baseless as they are?

When Spain became the mistress of a new world, she spread there her civilization and knowledge, she founded magnificent institutions of learning, still to be met with all over Latin America, in which the creoles received such liberal and solid education, that many from among them rose to the dignity of teachers and even professors. Cuba could not well have been gingerly dealt with in the plenitude of advancement of the present age, nor was this the case; on the contrary, from common education to doctorship in the most elevated spheres of learning, instruction is at the bidding of the studious, as is well-known, and the most obstinate of our adversaries cannot deny it.

Besides, all we have to do in order to prove it, is to give official data of the various centres of instruction to be met with in the Island. We can show that they embrace all the professional and scientific careers which may be selected and honorary examples abound to exhibit the good seed sown and the fruits produced. It will then have to be confessed, that what we have insisted upon, cannot be gainsaid.

Taking our starting point from so firm a basis and entering upon the subject in a spirit of serious investigation, the first and most prominent institution that will call our attention, is the University of Havana, whose programme of instruction, embracing as it does pharmacy, medicine, canonical and civil right, suffice to give us an idea of the general instruction there obtainable.

A chair of philosophy was there also opened up to the year 1863; but a new plan of studies, decreed by the government at Madrid, separated this branch of teaching from the superior professional, creating "ad hoc" a new school. Of course, the first director, salaried as he was, whom the national government placed at the head of the institute, was a gentleman graced with the cross of the order of Charles III., Don Antonio Bachiller y Morales, now a prominent individual of Cuban emigration, who declaims at New York against the *constant exclusion* and *benighted tyranny* which Spain has always been inflicting upon Cuba.

Adding, then, to these facts some names that have spread renown, and still do spread it, we think that we shall have done justice to the University of Havana. On consulting the "Guide for Travellers," we find, that from 1842 to 1865 the following have received the doctor title, among many other persons more or less known, and we point them out because of the character they have in subsequent events assumed in and outside of Spain:

Don Frederico Fernández Vallin, Don Ramon Zambrana, Don Joaquin Fabian Aenlle, Don Ambrosio González del Valle, Don Felipe Lima y Renté, Don José Ignacio Rodriguez, Don José Manuel Mestre, Don Francisco Fesser y Diago, Don Antonio González Mendoza, Don José Maria Céspedes, Don José Maria Trujillo, Don Francisco Zayas y Jimenez, Don Felix Giralt y Figuerola, Don Antonio Mestre y Dominguez, Don Luis Fernández de Castro, Don Jesus Benigno Gálvez y Alfonso, and Don Frederico Echarte y Gómez.

Some from among the individuals whom we have just named are no doubt worthy mirrors of their science and studies, and would not exchange their worth in the respective professions for that which the most renowned of this model Republic may have mastered. If, then, from these we turn towards other doctors, natives of Cuba, who are dedicated here to the medical profession to the general and just admiration of the public, leaving, in practical results, far behind them, a good many American medical men, what just cause does there remain for the assertion, that the pressure of a bad government stifles the intellectual development of the Island, as with levity some persons are known to declare, lowering their own mental acquisitions, and picturing an imaginary tyranny?

Let Arango, Gonzalez, Echeverría, Landeta, Gálvez, Illa, Adolfo de Varona, and others, answer in our place, and many besides who came here at hap hazard, some, perhaps, with the diffidence inherent to modesty, that they might be found failing in competition with Americans, and who, nevertheless, acquired enviable renown, and while doing so came to the conclusion that it was not precisely necessary to be American for the obtaining of the highest degree of learning and culture. Any similar impression of an apprehended insufficiency of learning is the most absurd that could be entertained in Cuba.

In order to corroborate this particular view, as regards instruction to be obtained in Cuba, we hardly need to dwell so much upon college education; all we have to point to is the ordinary run of well-brought-up people in the Spanish Antilles, who certainly will compare favorably with Americans similarly situated in life.

And are our creoles inferior to Americans in breeding, talent, general instruction, and the ordinary tact displayed in dealing with men and matters, or in whatever else of this nature?

From the alleged tyranny which, it is declared, smothers and brutalizes intellectual life in the Antilles, such results as we there perceive could hardly be expected to emanate anywhere, however much nature may have lavished her preference on both soil and climate to produce a spontaneously superior development of qualities as regards the instincts of a gentleman. Be it known, that in the Antilles the solid depth of erudition and astonishing development in the educational branches had long ceased to be the monopoly of foreign teachers, as they used to be in times past, but that both had fallen to the lot of the very creoles ere the Yara rising took place.

The superior junta of public instruction in Cuba in the year of the outbreak of the rebellion consisted of three sections, and the following were the gentlemen presiding: Don Ramon Navarro, a Peninsular Spaniard; Don Joaquin Santos Suárez, of Trinidad de Cuba; the Marquis of San Miguel, of Havana; Don Pedro Agüero, "poneute," drawing a salary of $3,000, of Puerto Principe; Don Francisco Alvear, of Havana; Don Manuel Fernández de Castro, from either Santo Domingo or Havana; Don José Silverio Jorrin, of Havana; Don Florencio Yébenes, we presume Peninsular; Don José Maria del Castillo, of Havana; Don José de la Luz Hernández, also a Cuban creole, and finally two gentlemen of whom we do not know where they hail from, Don José Guillermo Diaz and Don Ramon Hita. Secretary to the superior junta was Don Teodoro Guerrero, of Havana, who combined with his post that of chief of section of the supreme government of the Island, with $500 salary a month.

In other words, out of thirteen, ten were Cubans, composing the superior junta of public instruction, or better still, the management of education had, with few exceptions passed into the hands of natives of the land.

But, aside from the superior junta, the various cities of the Island had their local juntas and the following gentlemen made up the one of Havana: Don Domingo Garcia Velayos, of Santiago de Cuba, with a munificent salary adapted to his office of "canónigo," Don Ramon Zambrana of Havana, Don José Maria Céspedes, of Havana, who also drew a large salary in his quality of "catedrático," appointed by the government, Don Felipe Lima y Renté, of Havana, Don José María de la Torre, of Havana, Don Bernardo del Riesgo, we do not know wherefrom, Monsieur Emile Auber, Frenchman, Don Nicolás Azcarate, of Havana, Don José Toribio de Arazoza, we do not know, wherefrom, Don Antonio Ambrosio Ecay of Havana, Don Juan Francisco Chaple, from some other part of the Island, Don Vicente Martínez Ibor, Peninsular, and Don José de Villasante, Peninsular, secretary. Here, too, there are to be met with at least eight Cubans out of thirteen.

It would be more than is required and tiresome to go on producing individual instances in order to back up that which we are treating of; but one example at least should be given, the one, that out of twenty-seven professors of the University of Havana in 1865, twenty-four were natives of the Island, all respectably salaried. Among them figured names such as the following: José María Céspedes, Giralt, Zayas, González de Mendoza, José Manuel Mestre and there may be others, who soon after declaimed against the tyranny, the exclusivism, the ignorance and whatever absurdities else may have been imputed to Spain.

We have seen now, not only that intellectual life had an unlimited field wherein to move in Cuba, but that the spread of knowledge among youthful minds was specially delegated to whomsoever capable of doing so the Island contained, from the lower strata of elementary teaching to the very highest ranks of collegial erudition.

But this is not all. We can even show, that there was not merely the gloss and routine of instruction solely moving within the more generally humanitarian sphere of learning, but that there were professional schools, preparatory to every kind of calling, which young men might choose to embrace. There were professional schools for mechanics, surveyors, navigation, commerce, machinery and telegraphs, and preparatory ones for engineers of public roads, canals and harbors, mining, forrests, industry, agriculture and architecture.

All these combined, and with the professional school of painting, sculpture and engraving, also at Havana superadded, and it seems to us, that the Island of Cuba has little left to be envious, in the most important manifestations of intellectual life, of the most civilized Republic of the American Continent. How many Republics of Spanish-America will not feel humiliated before this loyal statement of the truth, at being left behind by *tyrannized and oppressed* Cuba in the true paths of progress and civilization, which the educational branch traces!

1

## XVII.

Another manifestation of intellectual life.—Harmony between the physical and moral forces in human nature.—Diversity of character and tendencies as applied to the investigation of social truths.—Political errors and personal fanaticism.—Their influence upon the pending Cuban question.—Fictitious complaints.—A question of political right.—Absolute equality between Peninsulars and Islanders in the Spanish Antilles.—The same in Spain.—Well-known injustice of the complaints.—Confined as those complaints are to a minority they fail in bearing a collective stamp.—The boasts indulged in, in this respect, form a strange contrast with Spain's real proceedings.—Reforms made in the Island during the past twenty years.—Convocation of a consultative junta by the government at Madrid.—Unmistakable influence of the step on public order in Cuba and Porto Rico.—Discretion of the national government in duly weighing the opinion of the majority of the junta.—Preliminary incidents and their natural consequence.—Public opinion.—The restless spirits.—Illtimed commencement of the revolution, considering that reforms were contemplated without it between the home government and the Cuban reformers—Pacts and promises —The fallacy of some—Apprehensions and consequent abstention of others.—Complete change of views operated in most of them.—The logic of the reaction.—Contrary arguments.—An answer reserved for the following article.

There are other manifestations of the human mind besides the fundamental one of public education; and one in particular has impetuously invaded the character of modern politics, with many and varied modifications, almost as many as there are individual tendencies reflected by the manifold traits which the physical organism of man involves.

With sublime wisdom God has rendered visible the divergence of passion, the sentiments and the mode of action of each of us, and thus while we do not meet with two human frames nor with two physiognomies absolutely alike, so that personal responsibility may cling to each individual, we observe the same diversity from a moral point of view.

From these eternal and well-defined principles, which

have not changed and cannot be changed in all the course of ages, for only God himself could change his own works, any just criterion might come to the conclusion that perfect truth applicable to the social fabric is a mystery outside of the natural order of the family precinct and the relation of the latter towards the wider sphere of public life.

This leads us to the inference that those, who pretend having discovered perfection as applicable to the political and social status of nations, are mere fanatics, self-adorers, a great deal more than reverers of that which they preach, for amidst passions and aberrations, only the most obstinate and extreme fanaticism can go such lengths as to claim for itself the privilege of having found out the true thing, for the so-called axioms of truth are so manifold, so contradictory, or lie so close together and present such a variety, that even the crudest errors are extolled as incontrovertible and unimpeachable truths.

Do not overlook these definitions, which are of the greatest interest with respect to what we are going to say, inasmuch as divergences arose, which transformed the country into two opposite camps, causing a portion of the native-born to rise against the bulk of their countrymen and the nation, and inasmuch as this state of affairs had for its basis rather aberration and personal fanaticism than any clearly perceptible shortcomings under which the intellectual life of the populations had been suffering.

Among the complaints which, for a long time past, had been raised against Spain by some dozens of men, impatient in their ambition, and by some hundreds of crudely ignorant ones, for purposes of changing from top to bottom political and social order in the Island of Cuba, was the one that has most prestige in the eyes of modern society without its being proved that either good or evil would result from listening to it. They put forward that the Island was deprived of right in the supreme Congress of the nation, and as, in fact, Cuba sent no natives to the Córtes, as the whole organization of its districts was not shaped upon the popular system most in accordance with the spirit of the century, the complaint was not devoid of reason, always abstracting from local traits not to be overlooked, which bring this question within the precinct of a distinction here applicable, for so far as Cuba is concerned, the Island is in an exceptional position, in many respects incompatible with the political and social order existing in the Peninsula.

There would be a more just cause for complaint if a line of distinction were drawn in Cuba between the freedom enjoyed by natives on the one hand and by Peninsular Spaniards on the other, if the rights of the ones warred against the rights of the others, if, in a word, the political and civil status, as between the ones and the others, were profoundly distinct, for within the folds of the same family and country a galling injustice might be thus met with. This not being the case in Cuba, but the strictest equality leveling positions, privileges and rights among all belonging to our race, without distinction of birth, and as by a tacit consent the advisableness was acknowledged by Peninsular Spaniards that in the imperfect political condition of the Island the introduction of the modern machinery of political organization prevalent in the Peninsala should be abstained from, and as the bulk of Cubans there were of the same mind, it is evident that reforms of the kind were not generally uppermost in the minds of the people, and that those who, inside and outside the Island, lay stress upon this matter, erroneously interpret the real popular sentiment upon this question.

And in taking this correct standpoint and summing up with it the statistics we have in a former article given as regards the comparatively small portion of the Island that rose in insurrection, the divergence existing there is at once reduced to a fraction of the people, and not echoed in its aspirations by the bulk. Dissidence is thus entrenched in open camp where fanaticism has raised the sword, but in the legal one of party differences we perceive no strife.

But Spain has never clung to exclusivism in her colonies, although envy has tried to belittle her glory and greatness and deny this fact, despite the circumstance that she filled her colonies with material and moral monuments ere Spanish America rose to consummate its independence. And the best proof has been furnished by the fact that not a moment has been lost, nor a single opportunity, to propitiate a more liberal course, in view of the high degree of prosperity in the Island, always anxious, as the men in power are, to improve the condition of the western gems we possess in all their sphere of political and moral life.

Hence, during the short interval of the last twenty years, precisely at a time when cases of hostility were shown that might have recommended the opposite course, Spain did not cease to liberally modify the administrative machinery in those possessions, but instead of remodeling from top to bottom every administrative and political department at once, the municipal reforms have been the first which, with wisdom and discretion, have been taken in hand, so that justice might have an even sphere from the very basis, thus laying the foundations for a provincial existence, leaving the future to carry along other welltimed reforms, and allowing the blessings thus gradually gained to ripen into fullness in another sphere.

Who can gainsay this? From the time that Don José de la Concha proceeded to Cuba up to the breaking out of the rebellion, there have been such thorough reforms made in the paths of positive right, the popular element developed to such a degree, the tendencies of the modern spirit were allowed such latitude in local juntas, in the press above everthing else, that there cannot remain the shadow of a doubt upon the mind of any one, that the government at Madrid intended to shortly raise the Antilles to the level of the other Spanish provinces.

Adhering, as Spain did, to this idea, she went as far as to call together near at hand a consultative body of notables, so that the reforms might be proceeded with all the more expeditiously, if such were feasible, having an eye to administrative reform above everything else. Was this convocation unproductive of results? Did not this very step show that there was a willingness to make liberal concessions so as to render more intimate the bonds of union between Spain and her western provinces?

Did not the steps sufficiently exhibit these progressive tendencies on the part of Spain towards her colonies? Was not there a state of transition rendered evident which should serve as a bridge between the long-subsisting and modern, throwing open to intellectual life the doors of suffrage, so as to enter a new existence which may be of questionable good, although part and parcel of relative progress in modern society?

This being the precise state of the case in which the initiative step taken by a moderate government was carrying the country towards a liberal representative regime, it is useless to go on repeating the blasphemy which ignorance utters when trying to justify the insurrection on the ground that the government of the Island was stationary.

The rejoinder might be made in this case, and not unjustly, that none of the reforms were carried out. The fact is that no agreement could be obtained among the members of the junta that was called to assist the government at Madrid and that without the support of a well defined course of policy as to what course would be most advisable to adopt, it would have been imperilling public order in Cuba, perchance, to act precipitately in the matter.

Prudence left no other course to pursue and events which preceded the calling of the junta recommended prudence, for there were two petitions presented, backed by signatures equally respectable, although some of them were affixed to both at the same time, notwithstanding the fact that the documents were radically distinct in tendency from each other, causing the government to hesitate as to the real wishes of the country.

What minister of ordinary precaution would have liked to assume the responsibility of acting upon a case which presented similar features of disagreement on its very face, the more so on learning that a large and respectable portion of the people had abstained from participating in the election of the junta, on the one hand, because they deemed the step an ill-timed one, on the other because they thought that the local management of the election was not impartial enough to answer the occasion?

And besides the aspirations towards public life are not participated in by everybody and there was evidently no necessity to precipitate reforms in the Antilles, where, to neither, the material nor the intellectual well-being, such refoms were immediately indispensable. Such reforms would have expanded the sphere of intellectual life it is true, but in a manner and at a time of doubtful opportuneness, at all events the way in which it was at the time manifesting itself in Spain was anything but edifying.

This being the case and aversion to similar innovations being already revealed among the greater portion of the community in Cuba, it is established beyond a doubt that all illegal tendency was of a partisan nature being *anti-Cuban* in the true sense of the word as shown by the small minority which backed the movement.

What shall we say, however, of the precise moment, when rebellion was resorted to, even supposing that the greater portion of the population had been bent upon reforms? In Spain a revolution had taken place altogether radical in the name of modern political ideas, a revolution which was actively supported by those Cubans, who desired reforms for the Island with the understanding that they should subsequently be introduced there also, as might have been supposed would be the case considering the course events had taken and as in fact they were introduced in Porto Rico.

And do not let it be said that the Cubans who sallied forth in the Island to kindle the spark of insurrection were carried away by the remembrance of the past, for the precedents of twenty years had sufficiently shown that there was a bona fide readiness to proceed in the path of reform, although more radical ones might prove injurious, a thing we shall not now discuss; and as for anticipations as regards the future, the necessary time had scarcely elapsed since the Queen's throne had been upset in the Peninsula, to determine whether or not reforms would be carried out, when the rising at Yara already took place.

That reflection akin to this must have got the better of the consciences of many Cubans anxious for reforms, is evidenced by the outspoken loyal attitude with which they sided with us from the very beginning of the struggle.

Upon some of the Cubans anxious for reforms ere the insurrection broke out the disloyalty of their former fellow believers has made such a deep impression, that they are not only the truest Spaniards, but that they even outdo their Peninsular countrymen and are now the declared enemies to all reform, whatsoever, for Cuba.

And this is perfectly logical and should cause no surprise, even though we may not in themselves condemn modern political tendencies, for rather than that the safety of the common country should be endangered by the extremes to which a sudden freak of caprice may carry turbulent men, traitors at heart, it is nothing but natural that men of good faith rather sacrifice as a matter of minor concern, reforms upon the altar of their native land, so that so precious a boon may be saved from the perils of unforseen events.

A delectable state of affairs, indeed, it would be, were a province to declare itself in open insurrection not only against the home government but against the sublime sentiment of the whole country upon the very slightest occasion!

Even men of less than ordinary understanding can hardly fail to perceive that the day is not yet at hand when artificial aspirations may be carried out, we mean men of common sense, who do not speculate upon the misfortunes of their country, or who do not live abroad to foster insurrection in Cuba, especially those from among the latter who do not stay in countries, where the sentiment of national independence has not been tinctured with abject money-making. Add to this the sinister prospect of Cuba becoming a prey within the claws of the Northern Eagle and it is clear that no Cuban who has his senses about him can lend himself to lowering the glorious destinies which a not distant future has in store for civilization in the New World, for the mere pleasure of persevering in bad designs that have brought about the raising of flags against country and family.

It is really not worth while that brothers should exterminate each other, while independence cannot thus be gained, when the only prospect at hand would be the absorption of the country by a race, exclusive in its tendencies, domineering and arrogant.

What would Cubans do if, after having rent by the sword the light yoke of the mother country, they found themselves chained to the ominous car of materialist American civilization, which adores the rich and distinguishes the strong?

By the force of routine some light scribblers tell us that the reason why that which happened took place, has to be searched for in Spain's exclusivism in distributing favors, and that in the spirit of partiality shown, she often irritated the creoles. The great majority grouped around our flag protests with its loyalty against so vulgar and mistaken a reproach. But since the word has been said and is so often re-echoed againt us, it is nothing but proper, that we should take up the matter and throw light upon it, so that no subject should remain unexplained that is to place our cause into its true position before the world.

## XVIII.

Privileges.---Unjust reproaches.—Their baselessness and the insolence with which they are made.—Cubans in office in Cuba.—In higher instruction.—In the administration of justice.—In treasury matters.—In the army.—In government branches.—General reflections.

None of the concrete subjects upon which light has been thrown in this work have caused us the amount of annoyance we experience in approaching that of preferential government employment.

Not that we were wanting in proofs to victoriously draw forth the truth; on the contrary, we are fortunate enough to possess more than sufficient, but their very abundance provokes our indignation on reflecting upon the lamentably calumnious system which our astute adversaries resort to every time they wish to surround their imputations with a halo of justice.

After endeavoring to disturb our family compact, after asking for our blood, we cannot bring ourselves to sit still and passively witness the unexampled impudence that characterizes them in endeavoring to palm off on the world their ideas lucklessly conceived, by which they make white that which is black, their aim being to make the best of a bad case, and in attempting to do so they display the inborn artifices of women, that have ever been deemed by us unworthy of men.

Whosoever permits himself to be beguiled by the chatter of Cuban emigrants who still perseveringly cling to the luckless insurrection, throwing back for years to come or sinking forever into a bottomless pit the future destinies of their country, will of course give them his sympathies, for under what tyranny does not Cuba groan? Have they not good cause for what they did, are there not abundant facts to speak in favor of the course they adopted? Have they infringed upon any noble sentiment when they threw off the mask? Is not there plenty of local adhesion, so that they may declare themselves the majority? What political and social virtues do they not parade about, so that their maturity for a distinct nationality and for the Republic be known?

And in the field, who is not a hero, although he may have sneaked out of the Island with the preconceived intent never to return? Are there any battles which ever they lost? And what laurel have they not plucked? Is there a glory that can match theirs in the history of the universe?

Still the plain truth is, that they are vagrant here and elsewhere remote from the Island, that their heart quails, that instead of being found on the field of battle where their metal would be put to a test, they made the best of word and pen to attain their ends. We should have to smother the consciousness of having sprung from a noble nation, we should have to be renegades from the generous blood which God instilled into our veins, if we did not sigh over the spectacle of the most degenerate sons that ever descended from brave ancestors, and if we had not the consolation to know that they have hosts of brothers that reflect honor both upon country and race.

However this be, a sacred duty demands that we should undertake to prove their errors, to use a lenient expression, in a manner best suited to the nature of this work.

They complain of the neglect in which the mother country kept them in the ordinary distribution of State offices, they say that they are shut out from careers, or at least from the *lucrative employs* of all of them. This is the precise expression, in which they indulge, and they add that they cannot fill the posts, although they may be obtained in Spain, because of the partiality, which they, at every step encounter, unless they serve in the Peninsula or in other distant possessions.

The reproach, or to use a milder term, the complaint, unfounded as it is, does them little credit judged from the stand-point of honor and loyalty upon which true patriotism should be based. We pity the patriots who have to lean upon *lucrative employs*, for the true notions of loyalty and honor should only be imbued with a disinterested patriotism, which leaves its imprint spontaneously, actively and vigorously, without the necessity of any other stimulus than the glory of our common country! But, admitting even that patriotism stood in need of a due share of employs while distributing the offices underconsultation of the budget and that Spain were the only nation that brought into practice a system of exclusiveness and discriminated against natives of the colonies, the laws in force in Holland, England and all other countries protesting against our applying a similar hypothesis to them, there is still such manifest injustice in the accusation put forward against Spain, it can be disproved by so many instances to the contrary, that the men who utter the same, can be but ill-informed, and the pen that commits this complaint to paper must be wielded by an individual of limited intelligence.

In article XVI of this series we said, that according to the *official guide of Cuba*, the professorships of the higher educational establishments in Cuba were filled by natives of the Island. That which we here repeat is so well-established a fact, that without taxing our memory, the following highly respectable names rise before our mind's eye: Messrs. Gonzalez del Valle, Zambrana and Valdés Fauli, all men of distinction, each of whom were rectors of the university of Havana during a lengthened period.

After thus proving the baselessness of the complaint so far as this most important class of offices is concerned, a branch in which any nation inclined to exclude natives, would, with an eye to what might happen, be applying the principle more particularly than in any other, let us bestow a moment's attention upon the law-courts and see what occurred with reference to them, Spain having in their case even put the widest construction upon subsisting laws, in order not to be in the least partial against natives.

The wise legislation of Spain provides, that nobody shall administer justice in the province in which his wife may chance to have been born, should he be married, and whatever the rank of a person may be, this exclusion is applicable, so that family ties and duty towards the people may not come into conflict with him. If the law were rigorously applied to Cubans, but few would be able to fill posts of the kind in their native land.

Is a strict adherence to the letter of this law that which we perceive there? By no means, for there was a time when in the Island all the "alcaldías mayores," or "juzgados de primera instancia," to use Peninsular expressions, were creditably filled by creoles, with very few exceptions.

Let the following gentlemen answer for us: Messrs. Palacios, Casanova, Ecay, Bustillo, Céspedes, Escobar, Vasquez Queipo, Toledo, and a hundred besides that assail our memory, all of whom would have been found to be incapacitated had the law been complied with to the letter; they could not have been judges, and yet they frequently filled the office of alcalde mayor, some, it is true, interimistically, but most of them were proprietors within the locality.

The supposition might here be arising that there may have been a short supply of Peninsular Spaniards, and this may have been the case in some localities, and, besides, these offices were comparatively of a secondary rank, but as even in the halls of "audiencias" in the Island, creoles have also been figuring, and in many instances, with great distinction and dignity, men born within the respective jurisdictions—none less than Mr. Vallin himself, Messrs. Armas, Cisneros, Valdés, Fauli, Guerrero, Montoro, Santelis, and many others besides—it is clearly shown that the infringement of the Spanish laws in favor of creoles has not merely been a casual and transitory occurrence, but that the breach came to be systematic, and fortunately justice was not the less stringently administered.

We say that justice was as evenly dealt as ever, for in an apparently criminal case of prevarication which led to a scandalous law-suit in the Island, it was precisely a native of Trinidad de Cuba, Don Manuel Toledo, alluded to above, who distinguished himself in his legal capacity. Let due acknowledgment be meted out wherever it be deserved.

But, why go on searching for examples merely among justices of the peace and ordinary courts of law, where even the highest grade, that of regent of the "audiencia" has fallen to the lot of natives of the Island?

Echeverría is from Havana, which did not prevent him from becoming regent of the "audiencia" of Havana and he was morever "regente territorial" of Havana.

We should be carried too far altogether, and the limited space of a newspaper would forbid our doing so were we to go still further back, for we should then be enabled to furnish proof that the list of Cubans is an interminable one that have been serving in the judicial career from "promotor fiscal" to "regente" in Cuba, to the utter confusion of those who talk of exclusiveness, while on the contrary we have broken laws to please them.

If then our defamers mean by *lucrative employs* those in connection with the treasury, they have neither the right to complain, for they have had their offices under it. All we have to do is to produce the case of Count Villa Nueva, who for years has been "superintendente general" of the Island, eminently to the advantage of the public purse and his own interests, and whatever complaint may be uttered after we have stated an instance like the one in hand, will of itself fall to the ground.

But, aside from this, we have the names of Las Casas, Calleja, Ramirez, Cárdenas, Jústiz, Carrillo, Mantilla, Valdés Hernández, Bulnes, Martin Rivero, Mallen and innumerable Cubans, who have held office of prominence in the Treasury of the Island, and if we sum up the names we have had occasion to cite, it is a proof also that our memory is not altogether impaired as yet.

Were we to undertake to produce other meritorious Cuban names in other branches of the Spanish service, we should have to devote a large space to it, but our columns are unfortunately circumscribed in extent. Who, for instance, is not aware, that our army teems with Spanish-Cubans? Who ignores that the distinguished and brave Captain Ferrer is a native of Havana and that during several months he has been Captain General of the Island? And who can deny the tribute due to excellence to men like Acosta, Ampudia, Villalon and other general officers who have taken share and still take share in the struggle on the side of Spain? Who is not aware of the enthusiasm, the decision and bravery of other leading military men, who, if less eminent than the foregoing, have not the less distinguished themselves; Portuondo, Romay, Laca, Bustillo Pérez, who, during the strife which this luckless insurrection has stirred up, have followed the natural impulse of the majority in their native land, who have proved a scourge and a terror to rebels?

Are not those who impute Spain with egotism in dealing out office perfectly aware, perchance, thát lieutenant governorships are confidential posts, and that they have been occupied by Herrera, Letamendi, Santaliees, Romez, above alluded to, and many others besides?

If all this be public and notorious, why, then, is the stigma of reproach still flung at Spain, a calumny which we have demolished by this article not through the instrumentality of an official array of figures, but by the enumeration from memory of a minimum portion?

It is not easy, it should be confessed, to muster patience

enough to be able to stand a system of attack of this nature, a system which endeavors to forge triumph from disloyal defamation, since by the ordinary legal course or by the sword it is not as easily obtained, because Cuba stands on our side, with the exception of so insignificant a minority.

## XIX.

Summing up from what has been ventilated in preceding articles, in order to prove that the independence of Cuba can neither be arbitrarily decreed, nor undertaken as an experiment.—Essential foundations on which it should rest.—Practical examples.—The colonial system of Great Britain.—The colonial system of Spain.—Respective results.—Necessity to be guided by experience, so as to avoid false measures ruinous to the future of the Island.—Statistics comparing the development of population and of material resources in Porto Rico with that of Cuba with a view to this question.—The number of inhabitants that Cuba should contain to be on a level with Porto Rico.—The population which Cuba might conveniently hold.—The two Islands compared with respect to their territorial extent and resources.—Digression showing their importance to the United States.—Necessity of retaining the Island under the Spanish flag, so that the same may reach the development which an independent state would require.—The eloquent examples of Hayti and St. Domingo.

We are now approaching the end of this pamphlet, for to make any further digressions would be useless. We have at length been able to produce a a batch of evidence showing the systematic dissemination of errors having reference to Cuban affairs by spirits either vulgar, passionate or ignorant.

We have pointed out to all true men the immeasurable damage which the rebellion could not well fail to inflict upon a country of the importance of Cuba, that such damage would recoil upon the commerce and revenue of the United States by whatever solution of the quarrel that might be arrived at now, which should not bring back the state of affairs in the Island to the same status that prevailed there ere the insurrection was set on foot. Facts in hand rather than by logical deduction we have striven to show the baselessness which underlies the scandalous proceedings, and by the production of figures that cannot be demonstrated away, we have furthermore shown that Cuba and Spain are a unit in condemning and warring upon such proceedings criminal from whatever point you may examine them, proceedings carried on by a handful of men who are still in the bush, and another batch of speculators without honor, without patriotism, and without conscience, who live abroad upon the spoils which events may turn up, without pausing to reflect upon the devastation which their mode of life produces in the land of their birth.

Cuba may become independent, but in saying that much we do not mean to imply that she will finally attain such independence while the spurious from among her sons continue to follow the lengths they are now going.

Even supposing that Spain evacuated the Island, or ceded it by a mistaken policy, and to the detriment of the general interests of the nation, and to that of all the mercantile and moral interests of the universe, there would be no independence, but merely a change of flags, that chained her forever in perpetual slavery under a more powerful nation.

We have fully explained all this in a former article, we have said enough to prove that it is not idle talk. Let us, then, fully and straightforward undertake a frank unbosoming upon the subject of our thesis with that sincerity which the work calls for.

In order to enable a colonial population such as Cuba has to aspire to the rank of an independent nation, it is requisite, if not as yet fully developed, that at least there should not be the capacity wanting, the proper development to attain it. To be deficient in such capacity involves the very greatest danger. Mere numerical force will not suffice to have the mastery of such danger, besides considering the extent of territory the numerical force that could now be mustered would be but small, and thus there could be no guaranties offered for the future as to the continuance of the country's advancement. Such advancement also depends upon its soil, its organization of labor, its morals, and its historical antecedents. Capacity for self-government cannot be decreed in a country like Cuba, we have to search first whether such capacity exists, by the light of science, the most searching inquiry must be passed upon it, so that all doubts be dispelled.

Let us point for an example to the United States on their obtaining independence. England had so weaned the colonies to look out for their own interests, their colonial education was made to such a degree that independence was, so to say, incarnate in germ in their official life as well as in their habits. They had been accustomed to govern themselves from the incipient stages of organization, their transition from the colonial state to that of sovereign communities was nothing but a natural event in their existence as a people, it was inevitable in any case, there was no danger lying hidden beneath their political, administrative and social habits upon emerging to a new life.

Spain, on the contrary, following the inspirations of natural sentiments, and being more concerned in the welfare of her sons, or, in other words, more of a mother than of a step-mother, has unfortunately not brought up her colonies to be able to confront premature independence; she has reared them to attain the development of the very utmost vitality near her bosom and in her lap, so that they may present themselves in the congress of nations on a footing of equality.

This loving conduct may have been a mistake, but it nevertheless is a fact, and should be accepted as such, for the hand of man cannot change in a day what centuries have wrought. For this very reason the independence of Spanish America has produced such bitter fruit in contradistinction from the brilliant results which the independence of the United States has brought about.

Taking, then, the things such as they are, and while some restless spirits would fain force Cuba into paths incompatible with the measured and progressive step of its organism, let us try to at least approximately get at a due estimate as to what our western gem will require in the way of advancement, to make her walk alone, the worthy compeer of sovereign nations.

We shall, in order to sufficiently demonstrate this last chapter of our thesis, not even step beyond our own Spanish Antilles in search of vouchers. Cuba and Porto Rico present them in abundance to enable us to draw comparisons and to finish up to satisfaction that which we have undertaken to prove. We shall, therefore, confine ourselves to them alone, and comprehension will be all the easier even among those who may be less experienced in researches of the kind.

Cuba, over an area of 3,615 square miles, had by the census of 1862 about one million four hund ed thousand inhabitants, while Porto Rico, two years previous, with 334 44-00 square leagues, counted five hundred and eighty-three thousand three hund ed and eight. There were thus in Cuba 386 inhabitants to the square league, and in Porto Rico 1,744.

Climate and soil being the same between the two Islands, as could be easily shown, and is besides sufficiently known to attempt demonstration under this head, it can hardly fail to strike even a superficial observer that a remarkable fact is here presented between the one, the larger Antille, eleven times the size of her sister, and the lesser one, nearly five times her superior in point of density of population.

We thus perceive that Porto Rico in the year above named had attained a remarkable degree of development as regards her population. She has since added to it another hundred thousand souls; but keeping in view, so far as Porto Rico is concerned, the census year of 1860 we find that the density of population in the Island was then as great, as that of the new German Empire has been found to be by a census taken after Alsace and Lorraine had been united to it subsequent to the late war.

What we have just exhibited with reference to Cuba, furthermore goes to show, that the Island is comparatively sparcely populated, and that, such being the case, independence is uncalled for. Not that during independence the population of the Island might not increase, were the same an homogeneous one and were there a better understanding subsisting among motley races. The case that would be arising there, as we have previously shown, would present another feature in as much as immigration would keep aloof and the material prosperity of the country, which now nourishes it, thrown into confusion.

We shall assume that Cuba may be strong enough to ensure the safety of autonomical existence the day she comes to the level of Porto Rico, but she would only reach such level on counting something like 6,304,560 inhabitants, at the rate of 1,744 to the square league, the Porto Rico density.

This would be, it is true, quite a large population and yet it would be but one-half of what she conveniently might hold, did she rise to the density of Belgium which upon 1,263 square leagues represents 3,928 inhabitants to the league.

In order to still better show the difference which results against Cuba in comparing the Island with Porto Rico we may as well take up again the annual trade balance of the United States, since it will admirably serve our purpose.

In the fiscal year ending June 30, 1870, the imports from and exports to Cuba figure with $71,000,000, and $11,000,000 those between Porto Rico and the United

States, showing that the larger Antille had a trade of $19,640 to the square league, against Porto Rico doing a business of $32,934 to the square league with the same country.

Let us now make a little calculation which it will do the American people good to follow us in. Supposing Cuba to be content to go on augmenting her population and wealth under the folds of the Spanish flag, the protection of which has brought about such results in the lesser of the two Antilles, so that she might reach independence under circumstances as favorable as those offered by Porto Rico at the present day, Cuba would appear upon the fiscal statement of the United States with the enormous sum of $119,056,410, which we arrive at on multiplying 3,615 square leagues with the $32,934 above quoted.

And in order to silence beforehand absurd remarks that might here be thrown in to try to convince us, that Cuba without the protection of Spain may be able to attain the same state of progression in the lapse of time that would be required to reach a population proportionate to that of Porto Rico, it is nothing but due that we should observe that the Haytian and Dominican nationalities taken together occupy an Island but little inferior to Cuba in size (containing 3,076 square leagues), while the population is 900,000. This population having at its command such a large and magnificent domain and a climate to match, have come before the trade of the United States with an aggregate of but $4,000,000 in the same year, or in other words the average to the square league was but $1,393.

Here, then, we have practical truths exhibited; theory before them is hushed.

Having arrived at the final demonstration which we had kept in reserve in favor of our thesis and which we intend should contain more substance than any of the preceding articles, our readers will pardon our taking breath in the meantime.

## XX.

The great slavery and labor questions.—Consequences of unconditional and sudden negro emancipation in Jamaica, Hayti and St. Domingo.—Logical deduc'ions from facts.—How slavery is disappearing in Porto Rico —In what manner it will disappear in Cuba.—Benevolent spirit of the Spanish laws, as proved by statistics.—New legislation.—Spain carrying out the great plan of labor reform without profoundly disturbing the subsisting organism.—Other changes.—Cuba's present population, what it may come to be in its greatest development and what population the Island will require for independence.—Statistical comparisons.—Numbers that tell.—When the change will be brought about in the natural course of events.

In the investigations which we have gone through in order to arrive at the definite clearing up of this problem, there will be found embodied facts of the greatest interest, not only justifying the reasonings put forth by us thus far counselling Cuba not to precipitate the steps of a measured advancement which of itself leads her to a glorious future, but also presenting a solution of other important problems that have reference to social changes in the Spanish Antilles.

In countries where the negroes have been emancipated without order and concert, the liberation of the slaves being the work of sentiment rather than of statesmanship, it has so happened that their number has been diminishing, like, for instance, in Jamaica, to an alarming extent, or that for purposes of labor and civilization their number counts for very little, as we observe in the case of Hayti and St. Domingo.

The natural conclusion from all this has been, and EL CRONISTA has accepted and sustained it many a time, that unconditional liberation is prejudicial to the slaves themselves, and that nothing would be more contrary to the legitimate interests of civilization and commerce than to knock off the shackles at a single blow, this all the more in Cuba where the slaves are still so numerous.

The abyss which apparently separates this argument from generally accepted modern ideas is by no means so wide a gap as many would pursuade us were the case, nor is it so very difficult to fill it as extreme philanthropy preaches.

If the Southern States of the American Union had abstained from transferring the question to the battle-field, no decree of instantaneous emancipation would have been issued Or do the philanthropists think, perchance, that it is more conducive to the good of a country to ruin it together with its workmen, for the mere pleasure of changing by a stroke of the pen the state in which these and their ancestors have been accustomed to live for centuries past, than to do the thing by degrees, to the manifestly greater advantage of the country, of the negroes themselves, and of the commercial interests of the world at large?

Porto Rico, where the emancipation of the slaves has not yet been decreed, offers the most conclusive and most praiseworthy example as to how the question may be and should be solved. All the colored people there were slaves at first, the same as in Cuba, the Antilles and Bahama Islands, as well as everywhere on the American main land, and Porto Rico contained in 1861 two hundred and eighty-two thousand seven hundred and fifty-one people of color, only forty-one thousand seven hundred and thirty six of whom were slaves, that is to say but about one-seventh. Since then the total population of Porto Rico has been augmented by one-sixth, the number of slaves has come down to below thirty-four thousand, and the precise proportion at the present day between the free colored and slave population of the Island is of one slave to every ten freedmen.

This miracle has been accomplished without in the least injuring either the moral or material interests of the Island and without inflicting a blow upon universal commerce intimately intertwined with the question, by merely two simple measures: abolishment of the slave-trade, come to an end in Porto Rico for many years past, and strict vagrancy laws. Free people of color are guarantied and imposed work through the instrumentality of certain municipal ordinances, which fix the wages and employ every freedman who may stand in need of work.

In Cuba, though later than in Porto Rico, the slave-trade was extinguished some years past, and there remains little to be said upon the whole subject. Let similar vagrancy laws be introduced against idleness and vagaboudry of free people of color and similar results will be reached in Cuba. Let the colored laboring classes multiply and become moral, held to useful occupation the same as has been ordained by Providence, that man should work instead of living like the Haytians do, or as the negroes do in the land from which they originated, to the scandal of the world. Let civilization disenthral the negro, lift him up and lead him to better destinies.

Our laws, even previous to those which the Córtes of Madrid voted two years ago and which King Amadeus despatched some months ago, have for their object the liberation of the slaves by a steady and progressive method, so much so that even in Cuba at the time when the slave-trade was still flourishing, and when the last census was taken, out of 504,488 people of color then in the Island, but 368,550 were slaves.

Add then the law enacted that all children born of slaves are free, and the extinction of slavery by age, voted by the Córtes and decreed by King Amadeus, and it is easily perceived, it is in fact as clear as the noonday sun, that slavery is at an end in the Spanish Antilles with the only exception, that instead of the fact being disastrous to the slaves themselves, to the Islands, and to the most legitimate interests of universal civilization, as had been the case in the colonial possessions of other European countries, and as it will continue to be for many a year to the Southern States of this great Confederation, Spain, taking warning from what happened elsewhere, will give the world the magnificent spectacle of creating in the western hemisphere a great and important nation by means of the very discordant elements which have scattered ruin around her.

If that which forms the objections raised by abolitionists against the measured headway made in this respect in Cuba and Porto Rico till both Islands reach the maturity of nations without undue precipitation were only the one that slavery is prolonged by us, the foregoing ought to set at rest this point, or the abolitionists are warring against the laws of humanity and logic.

If, on the one hand, the slave-trade has already been blotted out in our Antilles, if slaves are free at sixty years of age and if the children are liberated on seeing the light of day, no sophism can sustain slavery in the future.

All that is now left to show is to determine the period when the important transition may take place upon which this work of ours has been concentrating and we shall do so forthwith. We said that Cuba will have to reach the state of development in which Porto Rico finds herself at the present day, in order to enable her to attain without incurring dangers of magnitude, the rank of an independent nation, and we have at the same time shown by figures that this period may be reached by the time that Cuba shows sufficient development to count at least 6,304,560 inhabitants. This is one-half of what the Island may hold with an eye towards Belgium, a country not the superior of Cuba either in natural resources or geographical importance and in doing so we grant Cuba with the resources she possesses and the autonomical strength she may gather the same space of time which society grants to man, declaring him independent when about half of his term of life and his career has been reached.

By the aid of history and mathematics we can without losing many more words about it, easily determine the time when Cuba may be near reaching national emancipation.

Cuba entered the present century with an incoherent population of about 300,000 inhabitants, after granting refuge to families that were flying from Hayti and St. Domingo for their lives, and after the cession of Louisiana carried to her shores many from that portion of the Continent, and after Spain began to bestow greater attention upon the Antilles, placing the Island in a position which it was entitled to.

Between that time and 1862, the last taking of the census, the 300,000 inhabitants had increased to 1,400,000, being four and two-thirds times what they were then.

Assuming then, that the insurrection have swallowed all further increase between 1862 and the present day and applying the same multiplication above exhibited, and we shall have in another sixty years a population in the Island of 6,700,000 souls. In other words Cuba requires as an extreme 59 years to come up to the same density of population now observable in Porto Rico, and we believe that the country may then have reached a sufficient state of development in its provincial status, or if we are to give our own candid opinion upon the subject we would say:—

THAT IN ABOUT HALF A CENTURY FROM NOW CUBA MAY BECOME INDEPENDENT, THAT THIS IS THE CONCLUSION, WE HAVE ARRIVED AT AFTER FULLY AND SCIENTIFICALLY INVESTIGATING THE SUBJECT.

## WINDING UP.

Fifty years of the life of nations are like a drop of water in the unfathomable depths of the oceans and the generation, which is bent upon steering counter to the eternal order of nature is handed over to posterity branded with ignominy by history, after working the ruin of its own country.

This is our conviction as we write it down and we would rather that the hand tracing it should be severed from its wrist than that it should serve as an instrument to intrigue. If then there be mistakes in what we have submitted, they have not been premeditated, but are the failing of the scientific proofs we consulted. Nothing is infallible in human matters, nor have we the arrogant pretension that we would monopolize the exclusive truth. Have we not, alas! proved the truth but too much in that which in all sincerity we have demonstrated? We, therefore, but repeat what we said at the very commencement: let those who know it, show the truth, not merely by affirming that such and such is the case, as ignorance is in the habit of doing, but by means of other arguments superior to our own.

# APPENDIX.

## A MINE AND A COUNTER-MINE.

### I.

We are not in the habit of indulging in formal polemics with the *Herald*. Why not? A weather-cock that veers round with all the winds of the compass, mimicking the natural propensities of that which is vulgar in abject adulation of it, the paper will upset to-day its arguments of the day previous with the same ease, with which it will to-morrow with either fresh or threadbare aphorism destroy the most brilliant conclusions it may have arrived at in its last article.

The *Herald* is the incarnation of Penelope in the American press, the least reflecting of the world's press with few, and, therefore, all the more to be esteemed exceptions. We are at a loss what to be more wondering at, the daring with which it attacks and pulverizes the most solid principles of the social fabric and those of the organism of its own country, with no other impulse to inspire it than the wish to shine by insolence and extravagance, or the assurance with which it treats to its constant aberrations the American people, patient enough to listen to them, to applaud them and even to raise them to the skies.

We should almost be inclined to suppose that the one

were made to suit the other if events and their results did not turn up in a practical manner the real, the solid and true public opinion of the people, showing the little esteem in which the *Herald* is held and why the paper is nevertheless read. The American people is fond of strong emotions, as long as they do not affect its real interests, and inoffensive as the excitement is, which the *Herald's* tirades produce, the latter are taken in the same sense as theatrical display will be sought by way of relaxation in the midst of the graver daily labors, which keep it busy, enrich it and raise it to fame.

It is not always, however, our privilege, nor would it be patriotic in EL CRONISTA, to leave unnoticed the articles appearing in the *Herald*, for some of them bear a semblance of reason upon the surface of its organism and conceptions, which might inveigle those imperfectly informed, and since unfortunately solid and thoughtful judgment is not over abundant among the general public, it seems to us but due that we should prevent dimness of sight among readers of the paper in question by a quiet and reasoning answer, rather than that ideas of the kind should be adopted by Americans on the eve of the opening of Congress.

This is the motive which inspires us in reproducing here the article of the *Herald*, appearing in its issue of the 18th of November. Our mode of proceeding is fully justified and we are constrained to adopt it, reserving unto ourself a full reply to all its more salient ideas in the next edition of EL CRONISTA.

OUR FUTURE POLICY IN REGARD TO CUBA—SHALL SLAVERY EXIST LONGER ON THE ISLAND?

"The existence of slavery in Cuba is a reproach to the United States, and is especially scandalous to the Republican party, which has held control of the government for the past twelve years, and has just secured a new lease of power through the personal strength and popularity of President Grant. The crusade against slavery within our own borders brought on the war of the Southern rebellion, cost the nation hundreds of thousands of lives and millions of treasure, and still keeps a large section of the country stripped of those rights guarantied to all the States by the constitution. The responsibility of abolitionism for the war has been from time to time denied for political effect; but the day has gone by for such sophistry and the truth of history vindicates itself. When Mr. Seward, pending the first election of Mr. Lincoln, declared that the triumph of the latter would enable the Republican party within four years to convert the Supreme Court of the United States into a partisan tribunal that would interpret the national constitution as giving no rights to slavery, he committed an act of war just as effectually as did the rebels when they fired the first gun on Sumter. From that moment an appeal to arms became inevitable, and slavery in the United States was doomed. No unprejudiced person now thinks of upbraiding republicanism for its attack upon the 'institution' any more than they would blame the colonists who threw the tea overboard in Boston harbor. The end justified the means. But it is questionable whether a party that has carried a great moral idea to a successful issue at home at such enormous risk and sacrifice; that has soaked its own soil with the blood of its best citizens in the cause of freedom for the negro race, can, without censure, refrain from using its power to strike down slavery in the neighboring Island of Cuba. Yet we find our Republican Congress and the administration at Washington not only abstaining from aggressive acts against the system of slavery in the Spanish colony, but doing much to foster it and keep it in existence. We contend that inasmuch as the party in absolute control of the legislative and executive branches of the government achieved power on the principle of unceasing war against slavery as a great human wrong, it has not the moral right to remain inactive while four hundred thousand negroes are held in bondage on an island lying in our waters and within reach of our hands. Inaction is not, however, the least of its sins. The policy of the dominant party has given direct aid to Cuban slavery, both in its unfriendliness towars the cause of the revolutionists and in its liberal encouragement of Spanish interests in its commercial intercourse with that nation.

"We pointed out to General Grant a few days ago the fact that the shortest and surest way to liberate the Cuban slaves is to free the Island from Spanish rule. Independence to Cuba means freedom to every human being on the Island, for the regularly adopted constitution of the Republic declares that 'all the inhabitants,' of whatever race or color, shall be 'absolutely free.' The recognition by the United States of the belligerency of the revolutionists—a recognition to which over four years' successful resistance to Spanish authority entitle them, would speedily close the struggle and drive the Spaniards from the Island. This is the judgment of reflecting friends of the patriots, and the unceasing intrigues of the Spanish authorities to prevent such action on the part of our government indicate that they share the opinion. By refusing to Cubans, after four years of rebellion, the rights that were accorded to the South almost as soon as they had raised the banner of insurrection, our government incurs a grave responsibility, of which it ought to be glad to relieve itself, and, as we have heretofore shown, General Grant has now a happy opportunity to make a new departure in his Cuban policy appear a graceful concession to the sentiment of the people who have just re-elected him to the Presidency of the United States by a largely non-partisan vote. Should there be any hesitation about the recognition of Cuban belligerency, or should such action as we believe ought to be taken by the administration fail in securing the desired object, we have still the resort of an earnest appeal to the Spanish government for the abolition of human servitude on the Island, and, better still, the means of forcing that concession from Spain if we are serious in demanding it. Up to the present time there has been much talk at Madrid about the emancipation of the slaves in the colonies, and the Republican party has declared in favor of such a policy; but the promises of the government appear to have been induced by expediency and the declarations of the republicans seem to have been made more for effect than from principle. The protracted rebellion afforded a favorable opportunity for sweeping away the evil of slavery, had the Spaniards been really desirous of accomplishing that professed object; but so much time has been wasted over unsatisfactory propositions for gradual emancipation and so many difficulties have constantly appeared in the way of action that all faith in the sincerity of the movement has been destroyed.

"Intervention with Spain for the liberation of Cuban slaves is no new proposition to Congress or the administration. Neither has been idle in this direction, so far as sentiment is concerned. President Grant has alluded to the subject time and again; Congress has resolved and memorialized, and Secretary Fish has been as strong in words and as weak in action as usual. Congress long since adopted a resolution declaring that the existence of slavery in Cuba would have an important bearing on the diplomatic and commercial relations of the two countries, and notice to that effect is supposed to have been given by our

Secretary of State to the Spanish government. We have plenty of evidence to show that the powers at Madrid stand pledged to our government to abolish slavery on the island, a promise which they have as yet shown no sincere intention of redeeming. In January, 1870, Secretary Fish, writing to the United States Minister in Spain, said, 'This government regards the government of Madrid as committed to the abolition of slavery in Cuba;' and the Secretary went on to instruct the Minister that if it should appear that the Cuban insurrection was regarded by the Spanish authorities as finally and completely suppressed, he would seize the opportunity to inform that this government, relying on 'assurances so repeatedly given,' would expect immediate steps to be taken for the emancipation of the slaves in the Spanish colonies. In June, 1870, Senator Sumner presented a report from the Committee on Foreign Relations of the Senate, declaring the 'pain of the American government at the fact that the pretension of property in man is still upheld in the island colonies of Spain lying in American waters; that such a spectacle is justly offensive to all who love republican institutions, and especially to the United States, who now, in the name of justice and for the sake of good neighborhood, ask that slavery shall cease there at once.' In July, 1870, the correspondence between Secretary Fish and our Minister at Madrid was sent in to the Senate, and from that it appeared that in June preceding, about the time the above report was made, the Secretary addressed an official communication to the Minister, in which he spoke of the plan proposed in the Spanish Cortes for the 'extirpation of this blot upon the civilization of America' as falling far short of what the American people 'had a right to expect.' Mr. Fish showed at length the insufficiency and deception of the proposal for a gradual emancipation of the Cuban slaves, and said, 'You will state to the Spanish government, in a friendly but decided manner, that this government is disappointed in this project; that it fails to meet the expectations that have been raised by the various conversations with you; that in the opinion of the President it will produce dissatisfaction throughout the civilized world, that is looking to see liberty as the universal law of labor; that it will fail to satisfy or to pacify Cuba; that peace, if restored, can be maintained only by force so long as slavery exists, and that our proximity to that island and our intimate relations with it give us a deep interest in its welfare, and justify the expression of our earnest desire to see prevail the policy which we believe calculated to restore its peace and give it permanent prosperity.' These were certainly brave words; but they have unfortunately been unproductive of good. It is now nearly three years since they were penned, and Cuba is still in revolution and the fetters cling to the limbs of four hundred thousand negroes on the island as cruelly as ever. This is not as it should be. A powerful nation like the United States should utter no threat that it does not mean to carry out, and should make no demand that it does not intend to enforce. The republican Congress, which, nearly three years ago, 'in the name of justice and for the sake of good neighborhood,' asked of Spain that Cuban slavery should cease at once, and which declared that the non-emancipation of the slaves on the Island would influence our diplomatic and commercial intercourse with the Spanish nation, is the republican Congress of to-day, with a powerful majority in both branches of the national Legislature. The administration which nearly three years ago declared that the government of Spain was pledged to us for the abolition of slavery in Cuba; which declared that our government, relying on pledges repeatedly given, would expect the immediate emancipation of the slaves in the Spanish colonies; which formally expressed dissatisfaction with a scheme of gradual emancipation, and in view of our proximity to Cuba and our intimate relations with the Island pressed for the redemption of the promises of unconditional emancipation, is the administration now in power and about to enter upon a new term of office. Are the republican Congress, the republican administration and the republican party to stand idly by another four years, contented with high-sounding protests, while the Cuban negroes drag out their lives in bondage and suffering?

"There is an easy way to force the abolition of Cuban slavery from the Spanish government without the argument of powder and steel. The government and people of the United States are in fact to-day its chief support, and without their aid human servitude would not survive a year. Our trade makes slavery profitable on the Island; our money enriches the slave owner and confirms him in his desire to rob the negroes of their labor; the revenue we secure to Cuba make its ownership valuable to Spain, and raises up a barrier to its independence and freedom. In 1868, of the whole six hundred and twenty thousand tons f sugar exported from the Island in nine months only, from January 1 to September 30, the United States took nearly four hundred thousand tons, and during the same period, of three hundred and thirty thousand tons of molasses, we took nearly two hundred and twenty thousand tons. The sugar crop for the year 1870-71 was five hundred and forty thousand tons, of which the United States received three hundred and twenty thousand tons. We may safely state that we consume on an average between sixty and seventy per cent. of the Cuba crop of sugar and a greater percentage of the crop of molasses. This slave-labor sugar, under our present tariff, comes in direct conflict with our free labor, and realizes to the Cubans a larger profit than our own citizens can secure. On the other hand, Spain affords us no facilities or advantages in the Cuban markets. Her tariff discriminates against American imports, and the enormous duties are prohibitory of a great part of our products. Machinery and a few articles that cannot well be procured from home are the only things on which Spanish tariff allows us a fair market in Cuba. Our government thus directly encourages the manufacture of slave products in our immediate neighborhood, and gives life to the system of slave labor. If we were to place a duty of one hundred per cent. on the slave labor sugars of Cuba we should at once do much to loosen the hold of Spain upon the Island and to strike the fetters from the limbs of the slaves. The loss of the American markets would be fatal to the present condition of affairs, and it would not be long before the Island obtained its freedom or voluntarily sought an asylum within the Union. At all events, it is a policy which should commend itself to Republicans, unless their concern for the liberty of the negro has ceased with the enfranchisement of those of the race whose ballots are cast in the United States. At present the party which for the sake of abolition provoked the war of the rebellion stands in the position of encouraging slavery on territory lying at our very threshold; of placing foreign slave labor in competition with our own free labor; of raising no hand to release four hundred thousand neighboring negroes from the most cruel bondage. Let us see whether President Grant will suffer the Spanish government to trifle with us on the subject of Cuban slavery for another four years, or whether he will boldly take the initiatory in carrying into practice the policy which his present Secretary of State has been for the last three years so bold to avow and so incompetent to enforce."

Do not let the most sensitive readers of EL CRONISTA

be alarmed by the article they have just perused, for in reproducing the same in its integrity, we do so, as though we had been done a favor, and not because we feel in the least aggrieved by the absurdities it contains.

There is not one idea in it, not a word which cannot be upset and which we shall fail in annihilating absolutely and victoriously. If then upon this occasion we are to have the satisfaction greater than we ever had it, of producing such results, impelled by the very petulance of the *Herald*, would not the faintheartedness be great, which made us shrink from doing the service to our country at the very moment, when the American Congress is about to reassemble ?

## A MINE AND A COUNTER-MINE.

### II.

The argumentation set on foot by the *Herald* in the foregoing article may be and should be written against from various points of view, an article intended to induce the President of the United States to take a hand in Cuban affairs in a violent and decisive manner, inimical to Spain.

The first point of view bears upon the constitutional organization of this country. Although not the most interesting one to ourselves, it is very much so to the American people, unless the latter be resigned to fling its dignity at the feet of the first man of ambition, who may undertake to begrime it, while flattering the bad instincts of the crowd in the daring manner traced out by the *Herald*.

In order to bring out the hypothesis we have just dotted down in a more salient shape, we should fix our attention upon the call, which the paper addresses to the will of President Grant, inviting him to take either warlike or fiscal action, both of which are beyond the attributes of his office. The *Herald*, thereby, commits at least a twofold violation of law; on the one hand it aims at the relaxation of political sentiment in the American people, trying to familiarize its readers with the idea that the will of President Grant should be submitted to, and on the other tries to induce the President to exercise a disastrous dictatorship, which would be destructive of the true interests of his country, after trampling under foot the letter and spirit of the federal constitution of the Union ruthlessly and positively.

The eleventh paragraph of the VIII. section of article I. of the organic law, to which we allude, is so clear in its stipulations, that nothing short of Congress itself could change the friendly relations now subsisting between Spain and the United States, whatever the pretext might be, or whatever the question which the President might attempt to avail of, for the purpose of changing the said relations to do pleasure to the *Herald*. We dare not in all frankness determine, into which of two aberrations the said periodical fell, from the moment the constitutive federal right is called in question, whether the same purposely assailed the constitution of its country under the impulse of a bastard interest, not difficult to fathom, when we come to consider the perseverance with which the *Herald*, in its columns, over and over again takes hold of the same question, or whether it feels the necessity, that a foreigner should step forward to expound to the most popular and most widely circulated periodical in the country, the fundamental law of this Republic.

But, however this may be, a greater humiliation could hardly be inflicted upon the liberal spirit of the American people, nothing could more eloquently demonstrate either the bad faith or the ignorance of our New York colleague, whom we leave at liberty to take unto itself the one qualification or the other. And since regarding the other points of view, upon which we shall undertake to beat him, the said paper has been displaying neither greater fairness nor greater ability, we may as well give it as our opinion at once, that the "Herald," when it lost its astute and experienced founder, left a void in its reputation as an important paper, which there is not a second Bennett to be found to fill.

We have been often reading, with no small degree of astonishment, in some papers of this city the severe charges laid at the doors of President Grant and Secretary Fish as regards their international policy, especially with respect to Spain. We say astonishment, for while accustomed to study the laws of the country and the character of the nation, in the midst of which we follow our modest, but honorable profession, we have as yet been unable to gather from the American constitution, and much less from the practical life of the people, what legal and true initiative the executive power could seize, in order to stamp a personal character upon its line of policy in questions of this character.

It is true, that over this concrete point the "Herald"

extends its apostrophes to the majority in Congress, since the same originated from the Republican party, which, in a high-handed manner, abolished slavery. But who told the "Herald" that the measure would have been resorted to had the country been enjoying profound peace, a measure which President Lincoln took under compulsion of the all-absorbing circumstances attending the civil war, decreeing the same as an extreme step of salvation in order to rescue the Republic?

Real statesmen will not fail to perceive the true motives that guided the action of the Republican party at the time. There was no remedy left but the two proclamations of President Lincoln in order to save the Union, the one an exceptional one, and the other an absolute one. By a high-handed blow the war power of the South had to be annihilated. But there is the same difference between the case just alluded to and the raising of banners for the puerile satisfaction of destroying American commerce in the midst of profound peace, as can be traced between the action of the respective majorities in Congress while the war was at its height, and the one that might be expected to arise at the present moment without imputing to Congress the slightest want of steadiness of purpose in either its convictions or party leanings.

Does the *Herald* expect us to practically demonstrate to him that which we have just treated of? All we have to do is to beat him on his own ground, for if the majority of voters did not think like we do, they would never have kept in power a party that might be suspected of a readiness to trample under foot its very history and principles in the manner the *Herald* would fain have it do.

Seldom has there been so unequivocal a sign in a free community in favor of a prudent and peaceful government, as the one evidenced by the late elections; not only has this tendency shown itself in the reelection of President Grant, but in the crushing defeat which has been administered to the turbulent men, who in Congress have been all along importuning members with the question of free Cuba, as well as with the Monroe doctrine in a spirit very distinct from what might prove conducive to the true interests of their country. Greeley, Banks, Hall, Cox and other no less distinguished and influential republicans, who might have been supposed to be firmly seated in their respective positions, have, nevertheless, been ousted from them in the late election. Does the *Herald* suppose that if public opinion in the United States had chimed in with those men on the most concrete and culminating point of the article we are replying to, or even upon the general theme of the Cuban question, these men would not have come out victorious, although some personal split excluded them from General Grant's personal consideration?

Fortunately, however, the practical sense of the American people cannot be carried away by the idle talk of the *Herald*, similar verbiage in the press is tacitly disavowed and thus rendered nugatory; a distinct line should, therefore, be drawn between the one and the other, or we are liable to judge erroneously the one by the other and the result at the polls has been, although the *Herald's* boundless wisdom may not thus understand it, that the American nation, essentially an industrial and hardworking people, declines to entrust its future to dangerous adventurers, notwithstanding its apparent sympathy with irregular manifestations, a sympathy more exclusively due to free institutions and a liberal and tolerant spirit, than to the circumstance that any very great value is attached to them; at the polls, on the contrary, such irregular doctrines are in the end disavowed.

Had General Grant clung to his Santo Domingo scheme, or had he pronounced upon the Cuban question ere the late vote was cast for his re-election, he would certainly have been defeated at the polls. At it stands, the re-election is a flattering tribute of acknowledgment to the prudence which guided him during the first term of the Presidency.

There are in the article of the *Herald* contradictory phrases and charges intended to cast ridicule upon the conduct of President Grant and Secretary Fish, which, in other portions of the same article, are upset again; for if executive resolutions not having originated in Congress are forbidden by the law and they have on the diplomatic field gone the lengths submitted to by some Spanish ministers—as shown and affirmed by the *Herald* in exhibiting passages from despatches—it is evident, that instead of censuring, the said paper should have applauded them.

This we say with all the more candor, the greater the annoyance is which, what happened, causes us, for neither President Grant nor Secretary Fish, had a right to avail at the time of a critical state of affairs in Spain, in order to molest the latter with any undue exigencies, calculated to lower our national sovereignty, nor should a Spanish minister have listened to and complacently answered them, nor was there any occasion for the American government to take as a handle the assent above alluded to and to repeat that it was the promise of Spain—a minister not being Spain.

Does not the *Herald* thus understand it, when it goes down on its knees before the supposed argumentation of Secretary Fish, that slavery ought to be abolished in the Spanish Antilles? If it does, it knows nothing about the constitutional right of nations, and it acts improperly in arguing with such zeal, and so loudly and pedagogically, upon a subject it does not understand.

The slavery question is the war-horse now intended to ride to death our power in the Antilles, and the *Herald*, casting aside all further reserve in the matter, thus declares it to be in the article we have reproduced. And since the question is of the greatest importance, inasmuch as it affects the organism and the very existence of our possessions over the seas, is there any man half way familiarized with government affairs, who is not aware that without due process of law a change cannot be brought about in what is so closely linked with Spain? Tell us, then, where the legislative power rests in Spain; tell us where the limits of government attributes are laid? A question like this one would seem not to be out of place addressed to the paper of most repute in the United States, ignorant as it seems to be as to how Spain is constituted. Would not, on the other hand, Secretary Fish feel rather abashed were the question put to him with the exclusive character of an answer to his diplomas?

Spain is just as sovereign and as much the absolute mistress to take charge of her interests and her business affairs as the United States, and Spain has done with respect to the slavery question all that possibly could be done through the instrumentability of the sovereign legislation of her chambers, doing due homage to the spirit of the age, without thereby endangering her national interests, without inflicting a life of hardships upon the slaves.

Spain will never do what the North of the Union did to the South, disorganize its field labor and open the doors to pauperism. Spain has done the behests of her conscience, the dictates of her duty by unfettering labor by degrees, so that it may not starve.

Is not the law that liberates old men and the newly born children calculated to shortly carry out the abolition of slavery as radically as the most exacting may wish for? In four years, out of 350,000 slaves 50,000 have been liberated in Cuba and out of 40,000 in Porto Rico 10,000 by the same process of law?

What more do the philanthropists want? Whither would the absurdest exactions fain lead us? To general and unconditional abolition? Cast aside your hypocrisy then and turn your eyes towards the Brazils, a country holding 1,700,000 slaves and yet enacting a law of emancipation a great deal less liberal and effective than ours.

Why has not attention rather been bestowed upon that other piece of land on American soil, especially by the *Herald*, a paper that sends out its pilots to the centre of Africa for the extinguishment of slavery; why is Cuba singled out and diatribes leveled at her, why are threats flung at us, intended to overwhelm us with confusion and fear, threats which we laugh at. Why does not the *Herald* calculate rather who would be the loser?

Spain, we repeat, placing full confidence in the intelligence and management of the inhabitants of the Antilles has done what possibly could be done, and will do no more. Did not but a few days ago a telegram from Madrid inform us, that a certain proposition which had been started before the Córtes to abolish slavery by a stroke of the pen was shelved by an overwhelming majority? This ought to have sufficed the *Herald* and will certainly have convinced Secretary Fish, that it would be useless to base any argument upon what some minister may have promised in matters subject to decision in the Córtes and to none besides.

Although we, for our part, do not lay claim to statesmanship, we candidly confess that we should laugh outright the day that a declaration of war against Spain were forthcoming from President Grant *of his own accord*, that is to say, without being duly authorized by the Federal Congress: such, at least, is the idea we entertain of the attributes of each in his sphere, and the profound respect with which the law inspires us.

It would be difficult to imagine anything more silly than the threats of the *Herald*, and they certainly furnish us the due measure of its capacity and knowledge. The article being a leader, we cannot confine our thoughts to the writer alone, and, therefore, extend them to the whole paper.

The article says that a recognition of belligerency in favor of insurgent Cubans would be a mortal dart struck at the heart of Spain in Cuba, and that the American government should proclaim such recognition to be the beginning of the end to be reached.

An act of heroism, indeed, such action on the part of the

American government would prove to be! The act of recognition of a belligerent state would give us the right to search every vessel that seemed to us suspicious within arm's length of the American waters, affording us the full measure of vigilance, which we are now deprived of, so that we might then nip in the bud any expedition starting for Cuba, while American commerce would be hampered to the very entrance of its ports by the legitimate action of our men-of-war, and without any remedy against it. This will give an inkling to the *Herald* as to who would be the winner, and who the loser in the game, although some pirates might be benefitted by it.

This so much as material interests are concerned. Morally, the case would stand a great deal worse.

Fancy the pitiful part, which the American nation would be playing, were it to raise to its level a crowd of forlorn people, not even backed by their own countrymen at home! In order to enable the ambassador of the *Herald*, Mr. Henderson, to reach the residence of Agramonte, he had to go under safe conduct of Spanish soldiers, without whom he would never have got there, and a novel piece of humiliation it would be were the case to arise, that a minister accredited near the defunct Cárlos Manuel Céspedes had to avail of the good will of Spanish troops in order to discover where the power were located.

A recognition of belligerent rights calls for conditions which the Cuban insurrection does not possess: the first and most indispensable one is free and safe communication of the recognized Power "with foreign" nations, and neither the *Herald* nor anybody besides knows at the present day where in this world Cárlos Manuel Céspedes does reside, nor by what route he might be reached by anybody without forfeiture of life.

The fact is, that were a free people to be enlightened in the manner the *Herald* would fain do it, it would be irremediably carried back to ignorance and brutality.

Not without a feeling of weariness do we approach another threat, into which the *Herald* has endeavored to throw the balance of profound ability and wisdom still at its disposal. We might as well say that the worst enemy of its fame has maliciously slipped into its columns to let it shine forth the modern *Ecce Homo* of politico-economical lore, a nuisance to the criticism of statisticians of repute.

"In order to kill off slavery," the paper exclaims in a sublime fit of its fertile inspiration, "let us shut our ports to sugar, raised and manufactured by slave labor, by imposing a prohibitory duty of one hundred per cent. upon its importation."

And as so dark a thought could not decently be allowed to be based on thin air, the *Herald* falls back upon statistics, in order to show that three-quarters of the sugar and molasses of the Spanish Antilles are bought and used by the American nation. With this and with attributing to the tariff in force in the Island of Cuba the heavy dues which our colonial produce pays here, the *Herald* arrives at the stupendous conclusion, that Cuba will drop down powerless and surrender to its happy and overwhelming wisdom.

Upon examining the sugar statistics of Cuba made on a former occasion by Messrs. Zaldo & Co., Havana, it appears that the various crops produced the following yields:— In 1868, 711,000 tons of sugar and 265,000 tons of molasses; in 1869, 664,000 tons of the former and 234,000 tons of the latter; in 1870, 678,000 tons do. and 225,000 do. These figures differ a little from those of the equally excellent *Annual Review*, published at Havana, for it arrives at the following numbers:—In 1868, 749,389 tons of sugar and 259,011 of molasses; in 1869, 726,237 tons of the former and 247,050 of the latter; in 1870, 725,505 tons do. and 213,389 tons do., and in the same order in 1871, 539,441 tons do. and 152,459 tons do.; the *Herald* took its figures from the latter and we accept them as good authority there being but a trifling difference.

The *Herald* then goes on to show, that out of the above quantity 320,000 tons of sugar and a due proportion of molasses came to this country, and the paper finally comes to the conclusion, that if the duties on these articles originating from slave labor were greatly increased, the importation of them would come to an end and that the *coup de grâce* would thus be dealt to slave labor in the Spanish colonies.

In order to show the absurdity, which this argument contains, we are constrained to produce in our turn some statistics of great weight; like for instance the sugar consumed in Europe and the United States in 1871 and the enormous quantity which we contributed towards the supply by our privileged possessions.

The amount of sugar used during the said year was 1,927,000 tons, Europe having consumed 1,387,000 tons, and the United States, of imported sugar, 540,000.

Towards these 1,927,000 tons consumed on both sides of the Atlantic, the following countries contributed:—Beetroot produced in Europe 943,000 tons, cane sugar furnished by Cuba, Porto Rico and the Philippine Islands, 642,000 tons, and the balance of 342,000 tons by other cane sugar producing countries, excepting the States of Louisiana and Texas, whose crops furnished aside from the above 540,000 tons imported, the amount of 103,500 tons to the United States.

Spain appearing among the general sources of sugar supply under the head of her three colonies with such an enormous quantity, what does the *Herald* think would happen if the ridiculous prohibitive duties were to be imposed? We have it at our fingers' ends and shall let the paper know it: the sugar of the Spanish colonies would sell as well as ever in Europe, while the American refineries would have to shut up their establishments, that all the great industries which now thrive upon sugar in the United States would become equally defunct, carrying along in their failure many respectable firms, a large portion of the American merchant fleet would rot at its moorings in American harbors and finally the entire people of the United States, without ceasing to go on indirectly supporting sugar industry in the Spanish colonies by importing it refined from Europe, would thus only become still more dependent upon the latter, for possessing a *Herald* to give it its advice.

And what shall we say, if Spain were to imitate the line of policy traced out by our famous rival, and also adopted an indentical course by way of reprisal, laying such a heavy duty upon cotton, that Barcelona would cease importing 150,000 bales of American cotton annually, our spinners using Brazilian, India and Egyptian cotton, instead, and relinquishing for ever the use of the American staple?

Into another error the *Herald* has allowed itself to be drawn, when the paper said, that American exports to the Spanish Antilles did not amount to much. Upon examing the federal statistics of export for the fiscal year ending June 30, 1870, we find that out of $58,000,000, exported to the remainder of America with the exception of Canada, Cuba and Porto Rico received $16,000,000, without counting the re-export of goods, of which out of $7,000,000, the Spanish Antilles received $4,000,000 besides.

Add then the reprisals that would of course apply to everything of American production in the Spanish colonies and let us ask what will there remain of the important mercantile interests now linking the one nation to the other, the day that the government and Congress of the United States embraced the line of policy sketched out to them and urged upon them by the *Herald?* If the dagger is to be thrust into the heart of slavery, as from the good faith of the *Herald* we ought to infer, we are naturally led to the conclusion, that against Brazilian produce the same line of fiscal discrimination is to be adopted, being produce also raised by slave labor. If this be the case, let our colleague frankly state so, for American commerce also draws advantage from Brazilian sugar, coffee and India rubber and the great interests at stake in that direction are not to be left floating along at random, if the fiscal policy proclaimed by the *Herald* is to be adopted in the future.

And this is the paper that reflects the popular character of this nation, the paper that interprets its sentiments, the paper that educates the masses, the paper that exhibits to foreign nations American civilization.

The *Herald* in publishing aberrations of this nature heaps ridicule both upon its own importance and upon those who serve it. It misrepresents the American people instead of reflecting its true spirit.

This is the opinion we have arrived at, and with it we finish these lines, requesting the American people to read them, as their contents will not fail to be of service for the future.

THE END.

www.ingramcontent.com/pod-product-compliance
Lightning Source LLC
Chambersburg PA
CBHW022133160426
43197CB00009B/1258